CAVENDISH PRACTI

GW00375314

Business Tenancies

FOURTH EDITION

JILL MORGAN, LLB, M PHIL, SOLICITOR
SENIOR LECTURER IN LAW
UNIVERSITY OF EAST ANGLIA

SERIES EDITOR
CM BRAND, SOLICITOR

H.D. TALLAMY
DURSTON TALLAMY
SOLICITORS
26A HIGH STREET
CHERRY HINTON
CAMBRIDGE CB1 9HZ

Cavendish
Publishing
Limited

London • Sydney

Fourth edition first published in Great Britain 2001 by Cavendish Publishing Limited, The Glass House, Wharton Street, London WC1X 9PX

Telephone: +44 (0)20 7278 8000   Facsimile: +44 (0)20 7278 8080

Email: info@cavendishpublishing.com

Website: www.cavendishpublishing.com

Morgan, Jill
Business Tenancies – 4th ed – (Practice notes series)
1 Commercial leases – England   2 Commercial leases – Wales
I Title
346.4'2'043462

ISBN 1 85941 458 3

Printed and bound in Great Britain

Preface

This book contains an outline of the law and practice relating to business leases. I have tried to refer to original sources where appropriate and would emphasise that all practitioners operating in this field should consult the primary sources of the *Green Book*, *White Book* and the various statutory provisions wherever they may be relevant. Volume 22 of the *Encyclopaedia of Forms and Precedents* (published by Butterworths and available on CD ROM) is also an essential tool in this field.

It is a testimony to my predecessors, Christopher Hugill and Stephen Ford, who were responsible for the first three editions of this book, that a number of chapters are fundamentally unchanged. Thus, for example, Chapters 6 (Drafting the Lease) and 7 (Procedural Checklists) are very much as they were in the last edition. Conveyancers may soon be facing new challenges, however. The Electronic Communications Act 2000 finally completed its passage through Parliament on 25 May 2000 and the Lord Chancellor's Office has announced that he is likely to be issuing a consultation paper to obtain the views of the property industry on whether electronically created documents should be permitted. The initial proposals are likely to be aimed particularly at contracts for sale and mortgages, neither of which normally attract stamp duty. Electronically created property documents are the first step in what will undoubtedly be a radical transformation during the next few years of the way in which property transactions are carried out.

While the contents of some chapters survive, others have been subject to a significant overhaul. The introduction of the Civil Procedure Rules has made a huge difference to renewals under Part II of the Landlord and Tenant Act 1954 and have necessitated an extensive revision of Chapters 4 and 9. The Contracts (Rights of Third Parties) Act 1999 is dealt with in Chapter 3 but its practical implications for the landlord and tenant relationship are, as yet, a matter for speculation. Most firms seem to be playing safe and excluding the operation of the Act from their commercial leases so it may, in any case, turn out to be something of a damp squib in the commercial property context. We live in interesting times.

The forms appearing in paras 9.3.3 to 9.3.8 of this book are based upon Oyez forms and are reproduced by kind permission of The Solicitors' Law Stationery Society Ltd.

I have endeavoured to state the law as at 1 January 2001.

Jill Morgan
January 2001

Contents

10 Further Reading   159

1 Basic Information

1.1 Introduction

This book provides a guide to various practical aspects of business leases, focusing on their grant, renewal and assignment. Such matters constitute an important part of the work of the commercial conveyancer, but also feature frequently in the daily life of a general practice lawyer. Although this book refers more often to solicitors, it is appreciated that licensed conveyancers and legal executives may also be involved in this kind of commercial work. The term 'solicitor' should, therefore, strictly for the purpose of this book, be regarded as also applying to licensed conveyancers and legal executives.

Owing to constraints of space, knowledge of basic conveyancing procedures must be assumed. Readers who are unfamiliar with the conveyancing process should read Coates, RM, *Conveyancing*, Practice Notes series, Cavendish Publishing. They may also find helpful Brand, CM, *Planning Law*, Practice Notes series, Cavendish Publishing.

1.2 Sources

1.2.1 Statutes

Security of tenure for business tenants is governed by Part II of the Landlord and Tenant Act 1954 (the 1954 Act), as amended by the Law of Property Act 1969. If a tenancy falls within the 1954 Act, the tenant has:

- a *prima facie* right to the grant of a new tenancy on the expiration of the present tenancy; and
- the right to compensation for disturbance if the application for renewal is unsuccessful because of grounds (e), (f) or (g) of s 30(1).

A business tenant may also have the right to compensation for improvements under the Landlord and Tenant Act 1927.

Other important statutes affecting business tenancies include the Law of Property Act 1925, the Landlord and Tenant Act 1988, the Law of Property (Miscellaneous Provisions) Act 1989, the Landlord and Tenant (Covenants) Act 1995 (which modified the law relating to privity of contract and the terms on which landlords can grant consent to assignments) and the Contracts (Rights of Third Parties) Act 1999.

1.2.2 Delegated legislation

As with residential landlord and tenant law, delegated legislation deals mainly with forms and procedure and the most important are:

- Landlord and Tenant (Determination of Rateable Value Procedure) Rules 1954 (SI 1954/1255);
- Landlord and Tenant Act 1954, Part II (Notices) (Amendment) Regulations 1989 (SI 1989/1548);
- Landlord and Tenant Act 1954 (Appropriate Multiplier) Order 1990 (SI 1990/363);
- Landlord and Tenant (Covenants) Act 1995 (Notices) Regulations 1995 (SI 1995/2964);
- High Court and County Courts Jurisdiction Order 1991 (SI 1991/724);
- Rules of the Supreme Court (Revision) 1965 (SI 1965/1776);
- County Court Rules 1981 (SI 1981/1687);
- Civil Procedure Rules 1998 (SI 1998/3132 L 17).

1.2.3 Case law

The decisions of the courts provide an important source in this area and, in addition to the major law reports, specialist reports such as those found weekly in the Estates Gazette are essential reading. This is particularly important with regard to matters such as rent reviews and dilapidations.

1.3 Code of Practice

Following a consultative exercise on commercial leases carried out by the Government in 1994, a Code of Practice (drawn up by various bodies involved in the commercial property market) was introduced in December 1995. The objectives set for the Code by the Government were framed to:

- improve practice in the business relationships between landlords, tenants and their advisers, particularly when the grant of a lease is being negotiated and at rent review;

- encourage greater flexibility and choice through improved awareness of the alternative terms and conditions, which may be negotiable;

- promote greater openness and disclosure in the property market so that negotiations and the resolution of disputes, particularly concerning rent review, are conducted with the benefit of more complete and accurate information;

- ensure that businesses know more about how the market in commercial leases operates.

Recently published research, carried out by the University of Reading for the Department of the Environment, Transport and the Regions (DETR), has shown that the Code has proved to be of limited value: those who encounter it are the more informed tenants who already have a good understanding of the leasing process. Other tenants are not being made aware of the Code by landlords and their advisors, and unrepresented tenants have virtually no means of discovering its existence. The report concludes that it may be necessary to consider a move from a voluntary to a mandatory regime. There is a related code on service charges.

Because both codes are of particular relevance to small businesses, they should be read and noted by all practitioners operating in this field:

- *Commercial Property Leases in England and Wales: Code of Practice*, available from:

  RICS Books
  Surveyor Court
  Westwood Way
  Coventry CV4 8JE

  Tel: 020 7222 7000.
  Website: www.ricsbooks.org

- *Service Charges in Commercial Properties: A Guide to Good Practice*, available from:

  The Property Managers' Association
  c/o Accountability PR Ltd
  401 The Fruit and Wool Exchange
  Brushfield Street
  London E1 6EL

- *Monitoring the Code of Practice for Commercial Leases*, available from:

  Department of the Environment, Transport and the Regions
  Publications Sales Centre
  Unit 21
  Goldthorpe Industrial Estate
  Goldthorpe
  Rotherham S63 9BL

  Tel: 01709 891 318
  Website: www.detr.gov.uk

1.4   When to have a contract

1.4.1 Formalities

Section 2 of the Law of Property (Miscellaneous Provisions) Act 1989 provides that a contract for the sale or other disposition of an interest in land (which will include the grant or assignment of a lease):

- must be in writing; and
- must incorporate all the terms which the parties have expressly agreed in one document (or in each document where contracts are exchanged);
- may incorporate terms by reference to some other document;
- must be signed by or on behalf of all parties (or, where contracts are exchanged, one of the documents incorporating the terms, but not necessarily the same one).

Section 2 does not apply to leases of three years or less falling within s 54(2) of the Law of Property Act 1925 (see 1.5.1).

Particular attention should be paid to the requirement that all agreed terms are incorporated in the contract because the omission of a term will render the whole contract invalid. The use of side letters, to vary or qualify the terms of the agreement, should be avoided.

In the light of s 2, it is now difficult to create a contract to grant a lease inadvertently. Strictly, therefore, conveyancers need no longer use the words 'subject to contract and lease' in their letters. However, they may prefer to do so in their pre-exchange correspondence so as to prevent the creation of an express agreed term whose absence from a formal contract may invalidate it and to preclude any valid claim that a representation has been made binding by way of estoppel.

1.4.2 Grant of a lease

It is unusual for the parties to enter into a formal contract prior to a lease, unless there are special reasons. Thus, no lease may be possible until some event has occurred, such as obtaining planning permission for proposed alterations, or the head landlord's consent to the underletting. Alternatively, the premises may not yet have been built and an agreement is necessary to regulate the manner of their construction. In such circumstances, the precise form of the lease should be resolved and attached to the agreement prior to exchange of contracts, rather than to create potential uncertainty by providing that the lease will be for a certain term of years and rent and otherwise subject to the 'usual covenants'. It is apparent that these usual covenants can vary in each particular case (see *Chester v Buckingham Travel Ltd* [1981] 1 WLR 96).

1.4.3 Assignment

It is standard practice to enter into a formal contract prior to legal completion of the assignment. The contract may be conditional upon the landlord's licence to assign being granted (see Coates, above, with regard to the drafting of the contract).

1.4.4 Surrender

Where there is to be a straightforward surrender of a lease, there is little point in having an agreement prior to the deed although, if there is to be one (as with a grant and assignment), it must be comply with the Law of Property (Miscellaneous Provisions) Act 1989. Sometimes, a lease will require that the tenant shall offer to surrender the lease in certain circumstances (for example, before seeking consent to an assignment). However, an agreement to surrender a lease protected by the 1954 Act would be void under s 38(1) (*Bocardo SA v S and M Hotels Ltd* [1980] 1 WLR 17). The court may, on the joint application of the landlord and tenant (but not, it seems, before commencement of the lease), authorise an agreement to surrender a business lease (s 38(4)).

1.5 The need for a deed

1.5.1 Grant

A deed must be used to create a legal lease for a term exceeding three years (s 52(1) of the LPA 1925). However, a lease for not more than three years, taking effect in possession at the best rent reasonably obtainable without taking a fine, may be merely in writing or even oral (s 54(2)). Because of their duration, business leases are invariably created by deed.

Assignment

To pass a legal estate, an assignment of a lease must always be by deed (s 52(1) of the LPA 1925).

1.5.2 Surrender

An express surrender of a legal lease should always be by deed (s 52(1) of the LPA 1925). However, informal surrenders by operation of law are also effective and have been common in practice (for example, where the old lease has been superseded by a new one granted to the same tenant, or where the parties have wished to save stamp duty by not having a stampable deed. But see 1.9.3 for changes made by the Finance Act 2000).

1.6   When to deduce title

1.6.1 Grant of a lease

On the grant of a sub-lease out of an unregistered lease, the lease out of which it is to be derived and, where appropriate, all dispositions under which the lease has been held during the last 15 years must be proved. On the grant of a lease of unregistered land, the intending tenant has no automatic right to investigate the landlord's title to the freehold (s 44(2) of the LPA 1925).

Moreover, s 110 of the Land Registration Act 1925 does not apply where the superior title is registered, which means that an intending tenant cannot demand copies of the title. However, the register is a public document and the intending tenant can buy official copies of the freehold title and all superior leasehold titles from HM Land Registry without the authority of the registered proprietor. The open register avoids the s 110 problem for title details, but the Land Registry do not have a copy of every registered lease. Therefore, the tenant should also raise written inquiries of the landlord and inspect the premises to satisfy himself that there are no overriding interests affecting the interest which he is taking in the premises.

The tenant should insist in all cases on superior titles being proved, though the landlord may wish to resist this, particularly if the term is relatively short.

The Standard Conditions of Sale (3rd edn, SC) and the Standard Commercial Property Conditions (1st edn, SCPC) provide that, on the grant of a new lease for more than 21 years, the landlord is to deduce a title which will enable the tenant to register the lease at HM Land Registry with absolute title (SC, SCPC 8.2.4). In these circumstances, the freehold title will have to be deduced. The contract should be checked to ensure that (a) it is drawn up on the basis of the 3rd edn of the Standard Conditions/1st edn of the Standard Commercial Property Conditions, and (b) no attempt has been made in the special conditions of that contract to limit or exclude SC, SCPC 8.2.4. Otherwise, where there is a contract, the tenant's solicitor should add appropriate special conditions to improve the tenant's position.

The risks involved in not obtaining proof of superior titles are:

- the landlord may not have a good title and have no legal right to grant a lease;
- there may be a mortgage precluding leasing and the mortgagee's consent will be needed;
- there may be third party rights such as restrictive covenants and easements adversely affecting the premises.

If the tenant's solicitor is unable to satisfy himself that his client's user will be permitted, an express warranty should be required from the landlord to the effect that the proposed user will be permitted and, provided that the tenant complies with the terms of the lease, there will be no breach of any restrictions affecting the premises.

1.6.2 Assignment

If the title is unregistered, the assignor must prove the lease and all dispositions under which it has been held during the last 15 years. If title is registered, the assignor proves its immediate title in the usual way by office copy entries of the register of title and filed plan and a copy of the lease (see s 110 of the Land Registration Act 1925). The assignee's solicitor should always consider the need for a special condition to gain additional rights to investigate superior titles.

1.6.3 Surrender

There is rarely a contract and there are no rules as to what title each party must prove. However, the landlord will usually require that the tenant proves its title and, in particular, the landlord will want to satisfy himself that there is no mortgage affecting the property. The tenant should also ask for proof of the landlord's title.

1.7 Who pays the costs?

1.7.1 Grant of a lease

The landlord will often be able to use his superior bargaining position to obtain the tenant's agreement that the landlord's legal charges will be met by the tenant. This will usually be a term of the lease itself and, indeed, the agreement is not enforceable unless it is in writing (s 1 of the Costs of Leases Act 1958). However, on a renewal under the 1954 Act, the court will not order that such a term be incorporated in the new lease as this would deprive the tenant of the protection of the 1958 Act (*Cairnplace Ltd v CBL (Property Investment) Co Ltd* [1984] 1 WLR 696). When the terms of the lease are negotiated on renewal, the tenant's solicitor should argue, on this basis, that the tenant should not be liable for the landlord's costs. In fact, there is nothing to stop the parties agreeing that such a term be included in the renewed lease.

1.7.2 Assignment

It is unusual for the assignee to agree to pay the assignor's costs, though this does sometimes occur. The contract should also provide for who is to pay the landlord's costs for granting consent to the assignment. Both the Standard Conditions of Sale (3rd edn) and the Standard Commercial Property Conditions (1st edn) provide that the assignor will bear the landlord's costs (SC, SCPC 8.3.2).

1.7.3 Surrender

This is a matter for negotiation and much depends on which party most wants the surrender to take place.

1.7.4 Licences to assign, alter or change user

Where there are qualified covenants allowing the tenant to assign or underlet, to carry out alterations or to change the user with the landlord's consent, the landlord has the right to require payment of its legal or other expenses (s 19 of the 1927 Act) and this will be the landlord's usual practice.

1.8 Value added tax

1.8.1 The charge to value added tax

This is a complicated area. Guidance is given in HM Customs and Excise Notice 742: Land and Property, which is available on the Customs and Excise website (www.hmce.gov.uk) and from local VAT advice centres.

The general principle is that VAT is charged on any supply of goods and services where it is a taxable supply made by a taxable person in the course or furtherance of a business carried on by that person. A supply of land is made for VAT purposes by making a grant, assignment or surrender of it, or by accepting a surrender in return for payment. Taxable supplies include standard-rated supplies and zero-rated supplies. VAT is charged at the rate of 17.5% on standard-rated supplies and at the rate of 0% on zero-rated supplies. Some supplies are exempt. No VAT is charged on exempt supplies. Exempt supplies include 'selling, leasing and letting land and buildings'.

The VAT which a person charges others on making supplies to them is known as output tax. The VAT which a person incurs on supplies made to him is known as input tax. All output tax must be accounted for to Customs and Excise. Input tax incurred which is attributable to the making of taxable supplies by the business is set against the output tax to be accounted for in that business's accounting period. If such input tax exceeds the output tax in an accounting period, the difference can be reclaimed from Customs and Excise.

Input tax which is attributable to the making of an exempt supply cannot generally be reclaimed from Customs and Excise.

A taxable person is a person who is registered or required to register for VAT. Registration is compulsory if a person is making taxable supplies, in the course of a business, in excess of £52,000 per annum (as at 1 April 2000).

1.8.2 Election to waive the exemption

Until the passing of the Finance Act 1989, VAT was not charged on rents or on premiums payable on the grant or assignment of a lease. Since 1 August 1989, the 'election to waive exemption' provisions (more frequently known as the 'option to tax' provisions) of the 1989 Act have enabled landlords who let non-domestic buildings to elect to charge VAT on rents and premiums at the standard rate so that they can recover input tax on costs attributable to the supply (such as VAT on headlease rents or on solicitors' and agents' costs). (For a discussion of the effect on rental values see 5.4.3.)

The election applies to the whole building, including buildings linked together by a covered walkway and complexes consisting of a number of units grouped around a fully enclosed concourse (for example, units in a shopping centre) (Value Added Tax Act 1994, Sched 10, para 3(3)). The election will apply to all supplies by the landlord relating to the building. It is not possible, for example, to opt to tax rents but not a subsequent sale of the reversion. The tenant can elect to charge VAT on the premium payable on the assignment of a lease of a non-domestic building.

Once the decision to opt to tax has been made and notified to Customs and Excise, it can only be revoked in limited circumstances. Careful thought should be given before the decision is taken; it may make it more difficult to sell the building or to attract new tenants. The option to tax can be revoked:

(a) with effect from the date on which it has effect, provided that:
- written consent from Customs and Excise is obtained within three months from that date;
- no VAT has become chargeable and no credit for input tax has been claimed by virtue of the election; and
- the property has not been sold together with a business (or part of a business) which has been treated neither as a supply of goods nor services under the rules relating to the transfer of a business as a going concern;

(b) Where more than 20 years have elapsed since the date on which the option had effect if the prior written consent of Customs and Excise is obtained.

All rents which arise from the date on which the landlord's election takes effect are subject to VAT. If an election takes place in the middle of a rental period, the apportioned part of the rent will be subject to VAT.

If a landlord makes an election after the date of a lease, he can require the tenant to pay VAT in addition to the basic rent unless the lease prevents the addition of VAT (s 89 of the Value Added Tax Act 1994). However, if the election is made before the date of the grant of the lease, the landlord will not be able to claim VAT in addition to the basic rent unless the lease specifically allows VAT to be added to rent.

Most tenants will be able to recover VAT charged on rents and premiums. The main problems arise in relation to exempt and partly exempt businesses such as charities, banks, insurance companies, private schools and hospitals, whose ability to recover the VAT will be restricted. Such tenants may attempt to persuade the landlord to covenant not to make an election to charge VAT on the rents, perhaps in return covenanting in the lease to reimburse the landlord for irrecoverable input tax arising where the option to charge VAT is not exercised.

1.8.3 VAT and legal fees paid by the tenant on the grant of a lease

If a landlord grants a lease to a tenant and the tenant agrees to pay the landlord's legal charges, the landlord's solicitors must send their VAT invoice to the landlord.

The landlord is treated as resupplying the costs to the tenant and the resupply of the costs is standard-rated, exempt or zero-rated depending on the taxable character of the main supply of the lease.

If, for example, the landlord has opted to tax, the lease will be a standard-rated taxable supply. The landlord will issue his own VAT invoice to the tenant, requiring the tenant to pay the amount of his legal costs plus VAT. The resupply by the landlord is of the VAT exclusive amount, to which the landlord adds his own VAT. The tenant will then be able to recover all or part of the VAT, depending on the tenant's own VAT position.

If the landlord has not opted to tax, the grant of the main lease will be an exempt supply and the landlord will not be able to recover the VAT charged to him from Customs and Excise. The landlord should recover from the tenant the full amount of his solicitors' bill including VAT but will not be entitled to send his own VAT invoice to the tenant, because the costs are part consideration for an exempt supply of the lease. The tenant will therefore not be able to recover the VAT element of the costs it has paid.

1.8.4 VAT and legal fees paid by the tenant on the grant of a consent under the lease

If a landlord gives consent to a tenant to a transaction by the tenant and the tenant agrees to pay the landlord's legal charges, the landlord's solicitors must send their VAT invoice to the landlord.

If the tenant is exercising rights already granted under the lease for which the landlord cannot unreasonably withhold his consent (for example, assignment of the whole under most leases), such a payment of the landlord's costs constitutes part of the consideration for the grant of the lease by the landlord to the tenant. The landlord is treated as resupplying the cost to the tenant and the resupply of the costs is standard-rated, exempt or zero-rated depending on the taxable character of the main supply of the lease and will be recoverable (or not) by the tenant as described in 1.8.3.

If the tenant is seeking to obtain the landlord's consent to the exercise of a right under the lease or to vary the lease where the landlord has an absolute discretion as to whether to give such consent, the payment of the landlord's costs by the tenant is consideration for a separate supply by the landlord. This is chargeable to VAT at the standard rate unless the matter for which the tenant needs the landlord's consent is itself an exempt supply (for example, the grant of an interest in land, such as an easement, where the landlord has not elected to waive exemption from VAT).

1.8.5 Stamp duty

Where VAT is charged on rent under a lease, and itself is treated as rent under the lease, stamp duty is payable on the VAT-inclusive figure. If the lease provides for payment of VAT on the rent otherwise than as rent, stamp duty is charged on the VAT element as consideration payable under s 56 of the Stamp Act 1891. In either case, the rate of VAT in force at the date of the execution of the lease is to be used in the calculation.

If VAT may become payable in the future, for example, because the landlord opts to tax, stamp duty will be assessed on the value of the rent plus the VAT which is potentially payable. If the lease contains a provision in which the landlord agrees not to exercise the election to waive exemption, the Stamp Office may disregard VAT for the purposes of assessing the stamp duty payable on the lease.

1.8.6 Inducements to tenants

(a) Rent-free periods

Usually a rent-free period is not regarded as being consideration for a supply of services by a tenant but simply part of the negotiated terms of the lease (*Neville Russell v Customs and Excise Comrs* [1987] VATTR 194). There are exceptions, however: for example, where a rent-free period is offered in return for the carrying out of works by the tenant, the carrying out of works will be a supply of services by the tenant for a consideration equal to the value of the rent-free period (*Ridgeons Bulk Limited v Customs and Excise Comrs* [1994] STC 427).

(b) Reverse premiums

The policy of HM Customs and Excise has been to treat a premium paid by the landlord to the tenant (a 'reverse premium') as a supply by the tenant of its agreement to enter the lease and subject to standard-rate VAT. In *Cantor Fitzgerald International v HM Customs and Excise* (1998) STC 948, the VAT Tribunal had held that a payment of a reverse premium by the assignor to the assignee in return for the assignee taking an onerous lease was an exempt supply by the assignee. The tribunal took the view that the payment of a reverse premium in these circumstances falls within the exemption for the leasing or letting of immovable property in Art 13B EC Sixth Directive. Customs appealed the case to the European Court of Justice for clarification. Until a decision is reached, the assignee may choose not to account for VAT on such a transaction, or to account for VAT and, if Customs' appeal is unsuccessful, claim a repayment and statutory interest thereon.

1.8.7 Payments by sub-tenants to head landlords

The Law of Distress Amendment Act 1908 allows a landlord to claim rent from a sub-tenant when the tenant has fallen into arrears. The sub-tenant can, in turn, reduce the rent payable to the defaulting tenant under the sub-lease by the amount paid to the landlord. The landlord cannot give the sub-tenant a VAT invoice as the landlord is making a supply not to the sub-tenant but to the tenant, and the sub-tenant cannot claim any input VAT. Where the landlord has opted to tax the rents, any VAT invoice should be addressed to the tenant, who alone has the right to recover the VAT charged as input tax.

1.8.8 Surrenders

Surrenders where the landlord pays the tenant are exempt from VAT unless the tenant has opted to tax the property. 'Reverse surrenders', where the tenant pays the landlord to accept the surrender, are exempt from VAT unless the landlord has opted to tax the property, in which case they are standard-rated.

1.8.9 Variations to leases

Only minor changes are in fact true variations in which the existing lease survives. The effect of more fundamental variations, such as those which extend the length of the tenancy or alter the demised premises (for example, by renting three floors of an office building instead of two), is that the old lease is deemed to be surrendered and a new lease granted in its place. Any consideration which is received for either type of variation is exempt subject to the option to tax. However, where there is no consideration, no supply is seen as taking place.

1.9   Stamp duty

1.9.1 Introduction

Stamp duty is a tax on documents, not transactions, and in the context of business tenancies will apply to any agreement to lease, to the formal lease and to any counterpart lease. New rules have recently come into force as regards surrenders.

1.9.2 New leases, agreements for leases and counterparts

Stamp duty on new leases and agreements for leases is calculated by reference to:

- the premium; and/or
- the average annual rent over the term.

Ad valorem duty is payable on an agreement for a lease and duty is denoted on the lease itself. No duty is payable if:

- if the premium is £60,000 or less, with no rent: or
- if the lease is for seven years or less, or for an indefinite term with no premium, and the annual rent is £5,000 or below.

In the former case, a certificate of value must be inserted in the lease and agreement for lease, if there is one, which states that the purchase is not part of a larger transaction or series of transactions, for which the total purchase price is more than £60,000. If the lease does not contain this statement, stamp duty is payable.

A lease executed after 6 May 1994 will not be duly stamped unless it is denoted with duty paid on the agreement or contains a certificate along the following lines:

> We certify that there is no Agreement for Lease to which this Lease gives effect.

However, there are no penalties for late stamping of an agreement for lease, provided it is submitted for stamping within 30 days of completion of the lease itself. In practice, therefore, where there is an agreement for lease, it will generally be stamped at the same time as the lease itself. Only where there is likely to be a significant period of time between exchange of agreements and the grant of the lease itself would it be usual for the agreement to be stamped separately.

Any counterpart lease is stamped with a fixed duty of £5. If the landlord and the tenant sign both copies, one will attract full duty and the other a fixed duty of £5. Before a counterpart can be stamped, the full duty must be paid on the original document. If there is no duty payable on the original lease, then there will be no duty payable on the counterpart or duplicate.

1.9.3 Surrenders

A deed under which the tenant surrenders, or agrees to surrender, a lease in exchange for chargeable consideration (whether paid by the landlord or by a new tenant) is liable to duty as a conveyance on sale. A document under which a landlord agrees to the surrender of a lease for consideration paid by the tenant is liable to £5 fixed duty as a surrender under para 23 of Sched 15 to the Finance Act 1999. In the past, the parties to the surrender have often surrendered by operation of law in order to avoid stamp duty.

Section 128 of the Finance Act 2000, which applies to leases surrendered after 28 July 2000, extends the circumstances in which ad valorem stamp duty becomes payable on the surrender of a lease. Any document evidencing the surrender and any document containing a statutory declaration is now stampable. Where the lease which is surrendered is registered and no surrender document is produced, it is necessary to make a statutory declaration in order to close the title at the Land Registry. From now on, this will have to be stamped with the appropriate amount of duty.

In order to obtain the benefit of a lower rate of duty (that is, nil where the consideration does not exceed £60,000, 1% where it does not exceed £250,000 and 3% where it does not exceed £500,000), a certificate of value signed by the landlord and the tenant must be included.

No charge to stamp duty arises where it is clear that it has already been paid on another document. The lessor must show that a deed, written agreement or lease has been properly stamped. The document must relate to the surrendered property. In the case of a lease, the lessor must have granted the new lease in consideration for the surrender. Otherwise, at least one of the documents evidencing the surrender must be properly stamped.

1.10 Court jurisdiction

The basis of the jurisdiction of the county court was radically altered by the Courts and Legal Services Act 1990 and by the High Court and County Courts Jurisdiction Order 1991 (SI 1991/724).

There is a rebuttable presumption that cases of a value under £25,000 are to be heard in the county court, and those of more than £50,000 in the High Court.

In addition, the county court has jurisdiction in relation to applications under Part II of the 1954 Act (see s 63(2) of the 1954 Act) or for authority to carry out improvements under the 1927 Act (see s 21 of the 1927 Act) and rateable value limits are no longer relevant (1991 Ord, para 2).

The county court also has jurisdiction in relation to applications for a declaration that a licence to assign or sub-let, to make improvements or to change the use has been unreasonably withheld.

1.11 Glossary

Absolute covenant

A term used commonly in the context of covenants precluding assignment or sub-letting, alterations or a change of user where there is no express provision for the tenant to seek the landlord's consent. The landlord, therefore, has absolute discretion whether or not to grant consent in any particular case and can impose any conditions which he sees fit.

Arbitrator

A person undertaking a judicial function in resolving a dispute (commonly in a lease to fix the rent pursuant to a rent review clause on the failure of the parties to agree).

Assignment

Where the tenant transfers the whole of its interest to a third party.

Assumptions

A word commonly used to describe the terms expressly assumed in a rent review clause, helping to create a hypothetical lease subject to which a rent has to be fixed.

Best rent

The highest rent that can reasonably be obtained.

Break clause

An option in a fixed term lease enabling one or both parties to terminate the lease early by serving a notice to quit.

Clear lease

A lease in which the tenant bears the costs of repair, maintenance and general running costs of the demised premises, and therefore all of the uncertain expenditure, and the landlord receives a rent clear of such overheads.

Competent landlord

The landlord with whom the tenant must conduct the procedure for renewal under the 1954 Act and who is not always the tenant's immediate landlord (see 4.5.1).

Continuation tenancy

The extension to a business tenancy pursuant to s 24(1) of the 1954 Act at the end of the original contractual term.

Demised premises	The property forming the subject matter of the lease.
Disregards	A term commonly used to describe the matters which a valuer must ignore in calculating the appropriate rent pursuant to a rent review clause or on a statutory renewal.
Expert	A valuer making a determination relying on his own skill and judgment (commonly as to the appropriate rent pursuant to a rent review clause).
Fine	A premium or lump sum payment.
Fitting out period	A time during which a tenant carries out his initial alterations to the demised premises and, in respect of such period, a landlord may agree that the tenant can pay a reduced rent or no rent at all.
Fixed term tenancy	A tenancy which will end (subject to the 1954 Act) automatically on expiry of the agreed period.
Forfeiture	A landlord's right to re-enter the demised premises if the tenant is in breach of a covenant in the lease, arising where such right is expressly reserved, or where the lease is conditional upon observance of the covenants.
Headlease	A lease where the landlord has a freehold estate, as opposed to a lease.
Holding	For the purposes of the 1954 Act this means the demised premises, excluding any part occupied neither by the tenant nor a person employed by the tenant for a business (see 4.7).
Holding over	Where a tenant remains in possession at the end of the original contractual term, usually on a continuation tenancy.

Hypothetical lease	The imaginary lease created by the assumptions and disregards in a rent review clause upon which basis the valuer must determine the rent.
Licence	A personal permission to occupy land usually arising where the occupant does not have exclusive possession of the premises or in other exceptional situations. The main consequence of a licence is that the occupant has no security of tenure under the 1954 Act.
New tenancy	A tenancy to which the 1995 Act applies and to which, accordingly, privity of contract does not apply (see 3.2).
Notice to quit	A notice given by either the landlord or the tenant to terminate a periodic tenancy or a fixed term tenancy containing a break clause.
Option	A right to have some benefit (to terminate or break the lease, to renew the lease or to purchase the reversion), by serving a notice on the other party.
Periodic tenancy	A tenancy made for a period of a week, quarter, month or year and determinable by notice to quit.
Proviso	A condition attached to some term of the lease.
Quarter days	An annual rent is often expressed to be paid quarterly on the 'usual quarter days', meaning 25 March, 24 June, 29 September and 25 December.
Qualified covenant	A term commonly used to describe a covenant precluding assignment or sub-letting, alterations or a change of user without first obtaining the landlord's consent.

Rent deposit	A sum of money paid by a tenant or assignee as security for the landlord or assignor respectively for non-payment of rent or other breaches of tenancy obligations.
Rent review	The process of reassessing the rent at regular intervals during the term of a lease pursuant to the relevant provisions contained in that lease.
Reversion	The landlord's interest, whether it be a freehold or leasehold estate.
Root of title	In a leasehold context this is an assignment dealing with the ownership of the whole legal estate and equitable interests, containing an identifiable description and not casting any doubt on the title. The assignment should be at least 15 years old (s 24 of the LPA 1969).
Service charge	The cost apportioned between tenants of the landlord for providing certain services.
Sinking fund	A fund built up by contributions from tenants, and intended to be utilised for non-recurrent expenses and major items of expenditure incurred by the landlord and recoverable as part of the service charge.
Statutory renewal	The grant of a new lease to a tenant under the provisions of the 1954 Act.
Sub-letting	A lease granted out of a longer lease.
Surrender	The termination of a lease by agreement between the parties.
Tenancy at will	A tenancy which can be terminated at any time by either party.
Travelling draft	A draft document such as a lease, sent backwards and forwards between the parties' solicitors to be amended and re-amended.

Trigger notice	A notice served on the tenant by which the landlord initiates the rent review procedure.
Usual covenants	These are the covenants which the court will order should be included in a lease where specific performance of a contract for a lease is granted not specifying the precise terms.
Waste	Spoil or destruction of the premises for which the tenant will be liable in tort to compensate the landlord.

2 Time Limits

2.1 Grant and assignment

It is rare to have a contract preceding the grant of a business lease, although contracts will invariably be exchanged in the usual way on an assignment. The contract will most commonly incorporate the Standard Conditions of Sale (3rd edn), which also form the basis of the Standard Commercial Property Conditions (1st edn). These were issued in May 1999 for use in commercial transactions.

The table below summarises some of the more important time limits under the Standard Conditions of Sale (SC) and the Standard Commercial Property Conditions (SCPC). Although the terms 'assignor' and 'assignee' are used, the words 'landlord' and 'tenant' should be substituted on the grant of a lease, where appropriate.

Event	Condition
Assignee pays the deposit	No later than the date of the contract (SC/SCPC 2.2.1)
Assignor sends evidence of title to assignee	Immediately after making the contract (SC/SCPC 4.1.1)
Assignee raises written requisitions	Within six working days of the date of the contract and delivery of evidence of title (SC/SCPC 4.1.1)
Assignor replies to requisitions in writing	Within four working days of receiving requisitions (SC/SCPC 4.1.1)
Assignee makes written observations on replies	Within three working days of replies (SC/SCPC 4.1.1)

Event	Condition
Assignee sends draft assignment to the Assignor (no equivalent on grant of lease)	At least 12 working days before completion date (SC/SCPC 4.1.2)
Assignor returns draft approved or amended	Within four working days of delivery (SC/SCPC 4.1.2)
Assignee sends engrossment	At least five working days before completion date (SC/SCPC 4.1.2)
Assignor applies for licence to assign or sub-let	Either assignee or assignor can rescind if consent is not given or is given subject to an unreasonable condition by three working days before completion date (SC 8.3.4)
	Where the landlord's consent has not been obtained by the original completion date: (a) the time for completion is postponed until five working days after the seller has given written notice to the buyer that the consent has been obtained or four months from the original completion date, whichever is the earlier; (b) the postponed date is to be treated as the completion date (SCPC 8.3.4)
	At any time after four months from the original completion date, either party may rescind the contract by notice to the other if (a) consent has still not been given; and (b) no declaration has been obtained from the court that consent has been unreasonably withheld (SCPC 8.3.5)
	(NB: the SCPC require both parties to perform obligations in support of the application for the lessor's consent and while those contractual obligations remain incomplete the party in breach cannot rescind the contract: SCPC 8.3.8.)

Event	Condition
Completion	Unless agreed otherwise in the contract, 20th working day after the date of the contract (SC/SCPC 6.1.1)
Completion notice	Once served, completion must take place within 10 working days. Time is then of the essence (SC/SCPC 6.8.3)

If the period between contract and completion date is less than 15 working days, the time limits in SC/SCPC 4.1.1 and 4.1.2 are reduced proportionately (SC/SCPC 4.1.4).

(It should also be noted here that the landlord may not unreasonably delay granting consent to the assignment or sub-letting (1988 Act, and see below, Chapter 8).)

After completion, an application to the Inland Revenue to stamp the deed must be made within 30 days of the date of the document. An application for first registration is made to the Land Registry within two months of completion and for registration of a dealing should be made within the priority period of an official land registry search to obtain the priority given by that search.

Landlord takes the initiative	Tenant takes the initiative
Landlord serves s 25 notice given not more than 12, nor less than six, months before the date of termination stated therein, not being earlier than the earliest date on which the current tenancy could have come to an end	Tenant serves s 26 request of a new tenancy beginning on a date specified therein not more than 12, nor less than six, months after the making of the request, not being earlier than the earliest date on which the current tenancy could have come to an end
Tenant serves counter-notice within two months after the giving of the s 25 notice indicating whether or not the tenant will give up possession	Landlord may serve counter-notice within two months of the making of the tenant's request, indicating that he will oppose an application for a new tenancy

2.2   Part II of the Landlord and Tenant Act 1954

Tenant applies to court for a new tenancy not less than two, nor more than four, months after the giving of the landlord's s 25 notice or the making of the tenant's s 26 request. Service must take place within two months of the issue of the claim form and landlord must file an answer within 14 days (if county court action)

(See 4.5 for a more detailed account.)

2.3   Compensation for improvements

After the tenant has served a notice of his intention to carry out certain improvements, the landlord must serve a notice of objection within three months, whereupon the tenant may apply to the court for authority to carry out the works (s 3(1) of the Landlord and Tenant Act 1927)). At the end of the lease, the tenant must make a claim for compensation:

- where the tenancy is terminated by notice to quit within the period of three months beginning on the date on which the notice is given; or

- where a fixed term tenancy ends by passage of time, not earlier than six, nor later than three months before the tenancy comes to an end; or

- where a fixed term tenancy ends by forfeiture or re-entry within the period of three months beginning with the effective date of the possession order or, if there was no order, within three months of re-entry (s 47 of the 1954 Act).

2.4   Leasehold Property Repairs Act 1938

Where there is a lease of any property (save for agricultural holdings) for seven years or more with at least three years to run, then the 1938 Act (as amended by the 1954 Act) stipulates that, before enforcing a right to damages or exercising a right to forfeiture or re-entry in relation to a breach of a repairing covenant, a landlord must serve a notice on the tenant which complies with s 146 of the LPA 1925 and which informs the tenant of his rights under the 1938 Act. With regard to a claim for damages, the notice must be served not less than one month before commencement of the action (s 1(2)). If the tenant serves a counter-notice within 28 days, no proceedings for forfeiture or damages can be taken by the landlord, nor can the landlord physically re-enter the property, without the leave of the court (s 1(3)).

However, most well-drafted modern leases contain a clause providing that the landlord may enter the premises and leave a notice of any wants of repair. If these are not remedied by the tenant within a specified period of time, the landlord may carry out the works himself and claim the cost from the tenant. In *Jervis v Harris* [1996] 1 All ER 303, the Court of Appeal held that this is not a claim for damages and, accordingly, that the 1938 Act does not apply. It is not clear whether this also applies where the claim against the tenant is specifically described in the lease as 'liquidated damages'.

2.5   Rent review

Whereas the landlord and the tenant should make every effort to comply with time limits stipulated in the rent review clause, the general rule is that time is not of the essence and, therefore, the party failing to observe such limits will not be prejudiced. However, there are exceptions to this rule (see 5.3.2).

2.6   Options

There are three main types of option found in a lease:

- to determine the lease known as a break clause;
- to renew;
- to purchase the reversion (see 6.9.4).

The general rule is that time is of the essence with regard to time limits stipulated for options in the lease and must therefore be strictly observed (*United Scientific Holdings v Burnley BC* [1978] AC 904).

3 Privity of Contract: The 1995 and 1999 Acts

3.1 The Landlord and Tenant (Covenants) Act 1995

3.1.1 Introduction

Formerly, the original tenant remained liable to pay the rent and to observe all the other covenants in the lease throughout the whole of the term, even after assigning the lease to someone else. This is known as privity of contract. In addition, landlords invariably required assignees to enter into direct covenants with them in the licence to assign, so that successive tenants would also remain liable to the landlord, no matter how often the lease was assigned.

It became increasingly common for former tenants to receive claims from landlords for the payment of rent or compliance with other covenants under leases which they had assigned many years previously. Such tenants had no right to occupy and no means of mitigating their losses. The government took steps to remedy the situation in the Landlord and Tenant (Covenants) Act 1995 (the 1995 Act), while at the same time modifying the law relating to the granting of consents to assignment.

3.1.2 Old and new tenancies

The abolition of privity of contract brought about by the 1995 Act is not retrospective in its application (although, as described later, many of the other provisions of the Act are). Privity is abolished only in relation to leases granted on or after 1 January 1996 (these are referred to in the Act as 'new tenancies'; by implication, leases granted before 1 January

1996 may be referred to as 'old tenancies', and this terminology will be used in this book).

However, for these purposes, a lease granted on or after 1 January 1996 will still be an old tenancy if:

- it is granted pursuant to an agreement for lease which was entered into before 1 January 1996; or
- it is a renewal lease granted pursuant to an order of the court under the 1954 Act where the court order was made before 1 January 1996; or
- it is granted pursuant to an option where the option itself was entered into before 1 January 1996, even if the option was exercised after that date; or
- it is granted pursuant to a conditional contract where the contract was entered into before 1 January 1996, even if the conditions were not fulfilled until after that date; or
- it is a lease being granted to a former guarantor under the provisions of the surety covenants given by the guarantor and those surety covenants were entered into (whether in the lease or a subsequent document) before 1 January 1996; or
- it is an overriding lease granted pursuant to s 19 of the 1995 Act and the original tenancy was an old tenancy (see 3.6).

It is suggested that all leases granted after 1 January 1996 should state whether or not they are new tenancies and, where relevant, the reason why the lease is not a new tenancy.

A deemed surrender and re-grant of an old tenancy (brought about where a lease is varied in such a fundamental way as to create a completely new tenancy between the parties) produces a new tenancy which will not be subject to the old privity rules, for example, where the extent of the demised premises is increased or where the rent payable is increased (other than by a rent review provided for under the terms of the lease itself). The 1995 Act will apply to the new lease as a new tenancy, with the consequent release of an original tenant from ongoing liability. Another consequence may be the release of any guarantors or other assignees who have given direct covenants to the landlord at any time before the implied surrender. A tenant may have an additional liability for stamp duty on the new lease (see 1.9.3) and, if registrable at HM Land Registry, will have to re-register the lease. One way of avoiding such potential pitfalls is for the landlord to deal with an extension of the term by granting a reversionary lease to commence as soon as the existing lease comes to an end. Any extension to the demise should be dealt with by way of a supplemental lease.

Thus, it is now even more important than before to consider carefully the effect of any proposed variation since, if the lease becomes a new tenancy, the landlord will have lost the benefit of privity of contract from previous tenants and guarantors and the alienation provisions will almost certainly be inappropriate.

3.1.3 New tenancies only: the abolition of privity of contract

Release of tenants

As the abolition of privity of contract applies only to new tenancies, the old rules (subject to the changes described in the later sections of this chapter) will continue to apply to existing leases and to leases granted after 1 January 1996 which are still 'old tenancies' under the 1995 Act.

The fundamental rule is set out in s 5 of the 1995 Act: on assignment of the whole of the premises, tenants are automatically released from the tenant covenants of the tenancy and will cease to be entitled to the benefit of the landlord covenants of the tenancy as from the assignment. (On an assignment of part, the release relates only to the part assigned.) A 'tenant covenant' is one 'falling to be complied with by the tenant of premises demised by the tenancy' (s 28(1)) and a 'tenant' is the 'person entitled for the time being to the term of the tenancy'. Section 5 applies not only to the original tenant, but also to any subsequent assignee of the tenancy if a further assignment takes place. It will also release any other person, such as a guarantor, who is bound by the covenants in the tenancy, to the same extent that the tenant is released (s 24(2)).

It should be noted that:

- the automatic release of the tenant (or subsequent assignee) will not affect any liability which arises from a breach of covenant occurring before the assignment;
- the automatic release does not apply to an assignment which is in breach of covenant; or occurs by operation of law (for example, where a tenant dies and the tenancy vests in the tenant's personal representatives, or where the tenant goes bankrupt and the tenancy becomes vested in the trustee in bankruptcy (s 11). Such assignments are described as 'excluded assignments'. Where there is an excluded assignment, the outgoing tenant remains liable, but is released automatically on the next assignment which is not an excluded assignment;
- where the lease permits (for example, where the landlord's consent may not be withheld unreasonably and this is a reasonable condition), the landlord may call for the outgoing tenant to guarantee the

obligations of its immediate assignee. Such a guarantee is referred to as an 'authorised guarantee agreement' (AGA). The outgoing tenant's liability under an AGA must end with the next following assignment of the lease which is not an excluded assignment.

Authorised guarantee agreements

Section 16 of the 1995 Act specifically permits a landlord to require an outgoing tenant to guarantee the obligations of his immediate assignee by entering into an AGA. In circumstances where the landlord's consent may not be withheld unreasonably to the assignment, the landlord may only require an AGA where this is reasonable, but most landlords will wish to include in their alienation provisions a specific obligation on the tenant to provide an AGA if requested by the landlord. Tenants will generally wish to restrict this obligation to circumstances in which such a request is reasonable.

The Act lays down a number of requirements for AGAs. An AGA may:

- be given by the original tenant or by any of his successors;
- oblige the outgoing tenant on an assignment to guarantee the performance of any or all of the tenant covenants by his immediate successor;
- impose on the outgoing tenant liability as principal debtor in respect of any obligation owed by the assignee under the tenancy;
- impose on the outgoing tenant as guarantor of the assignee's performance of the relevant covenant liabilities which are no more onerous than those which he would owe as principal debtor in respect of those covenants;
- require the outgoing tenant in the event of disclaimer of the tenancy to take up a new lease for the residue of the term subject to covenants no more onerous than those of that tenancy.

An AGA must not:

- require the tenant to guarantee the performance of anyone other than his immediate assignee;
- impose any liability in respect of any period after the assignee has (lawfully) assigned the lease.

The following points in particular should be noted:

- the obligation on the guarantor to take up a new lease can, in relation to an AGA, only apply on the disclaimer of the principal tenancy and not (as is the case in many modern 'institutional' leases) on the forfeiture of that tenancy;

- some modern leases impose on the guarantor an obligation that, if the landlord does not require the guarantor to take up a new lease, he will nevertheless continue to pay the rent for a specified period. Such an obligation may not be imposed in relation to an AGA;
- it is fundamental to an AGA that the guarantor's liability under it will end on the next assignment of the lease which is not an excluded assignment. A provision that the guarantor's liability is unaffected by any assignment of the lease is therefore inappropriate;
- any provision that the liability of the guarantor is unaffected by any variation of the principal tenancy must be made expressly subject to s 18 of the 1995 Act (liability for 'relevant variations', discussed in 3.4).

Release of guarantors

Section 24(2) of the 1995 Act provides that a third party who guarantees the obligations of a tenant is automatically released at the same time and 'to the same extent' as his principal. On an assignment (other than an excluded assignment), the liability of a guarantor will therefore end at the same time as that of the tenant whose obligations have been guaranteed. However, this release applies only where the tenant is released by virtue of the 1995 Act, so that, for instance, disclaimer of a lease by a trustee in bankruptcy or liquidator will release the tenant, but not (depending on the wording of the relevant guarantee) the guarantor.

There have been no decided cases on AGAs and guarantors. It is unclear, therefore, whether guarantors can be obliged to guarantee the obligations of a former tenant in an AGA. It may be that any attempt contractually to bind the guarantor into guaranteeing any obligations of a former tenant under an AGA would be an attempt to frustrate or modify the intention of s 24(2) and would be rendered void by virtue of the Act's anti-avoidance provisions contained in s 25. Clearly, the landlord should not ask the guarantor to covenant to join in the AGA as surety. Nowhere in s 16 does the Act mention guarantee provisions and the insertion of a guarantee in an AGA may render the AGA completely invalid. Possible solutions are either to have the guarantor covenant in the lease to guarantee the tenant both for the time the tenant is the tenant under the lease and for the period of any AGA, or to have the guarantor covenant to enter into a separate guarantee document which sits alongside the AGA.

Section 22 allows the landlord to impose conditions on assignment; provided they are properly set out in the lease or other document in advance, they cannot be found to be unreasonable. This provides enough scope for making it a condition of assignment that the tenant procures that either the guarantor or a third party guarantees the tenant's AGA.

Until the law is clarified, the safest solution is to make sure that a company of substance takes the lease as tenant.

Release of landlords

Sections 6–8 provide for the release of a landlord under a new tenancy when it assigns its reversion. Unlike the release of tenants, however, the release is not automatic and must be applied for before the assignment or no later than four weeks after it by service of a notice on the tenant in the form set out in the Landlord and Tenant (Covenants) Act 1995 (Notices) Regulations 1995 SI 1995/2964. If the tenant does not agree to a release, the landlord may apply to the county court for a declaration that it is reasonable for him to be released.

If a landlord is not released when he assigns the reversion, he may again apply to be released on subsequent assignments of the reversion.

3.1.4 All leases: liability for relevant variations

Section 18 of the 1995 Act contains provisions protecting former tenants and their guarantors under old tenancies and former tenants under new tenancies who have entered into AGAs by preventing claims in respect of items not originally bargained for by the person against whom the claim is made. The provisions do not apply to the guarantors of current tenants.

The provisions relate to sums due as a result of a 'relevant variation', which is a variation of the lease:

- effected after the commencement of the 1995 Act and either:
- the landlord had the absolute right at the time of the variation to refuse it; or
- the landlord would have had such a right immediately before the assignment by the relevant former tenant.

The effect of the provisions is that a former tenant or his guarantor is not liable to pay any amount to the extent that it is referable to any relevant variation of the tenant's covenants effected after the date of assignment of the lease by that former tenant. For instance, if the lease contains an absolute bar against underletting and the landlord enters into a deed of variation so that underlettings are permitted with the landlord's consent, then former tenants and their guarantors will not be liable for any increase in rent occasioned by this variation, either at the time of the variation or on subsequent rent reviews. They will, however, remain liable for the rent which would have been payable if the lease had not been varied.

Where the variation was effected before the 1995 Act came into force, the situation is still governed by the common law. Therefore, if an old lease provides for some future variation of the tenant's obligations (for example, by a rent review clause) then, depending on the construction of the covenants in the original lease, the original tenant may be bound to perform the obligation so varied even though the variation occurs after the assignment of the lease. In *Beegas Nominees v BHP Petroleum Ltd* [1998] EGCS 60, the rent review clause provided for a single rent payable from the review date. It was held that the original tenant (and the intermediate tenant who had given a direct covenant) were not liable to pay a stepped rent on review (as had been agreed by the landlord and the defaulting assignee), but were liable to pay whatever was the appropriate reviewed rent from the review date.

3.1.5 All leases: time limit on claims

Section 17 of the 1995 Act contains provisions protecting former tenants and anyone else who is not the current tenant or the guarantor of the current tenant, by imposing a strict time limit within which claims in respect of any fixed charges payable under the lease must be notified to such third parties.

'Fixed charges' are defined as meaning rent, service charge and liquidated sums, but do not cover unliquidated sums, for example, a claim for breach of the repairing covenant. However, any sum reserved as rent (such as insurance premiums and Value Added Tax) will be covered.

Unless the relevant person is notified of a claim within the period of six months from the date on which the relevant payment fell due, that person will not be liable in respect of that claim. The form of notice which must be used is prescribed by the 1995 Notices Regulations (see 3.1.3) and an example of such a notice is included as Precedent 9.5.

Further, the amount which the relevant person is liable to pay cannot exceed the amount specified in the notice, unless the notice warned the person of that possibility and the landlord serves a further notice (also prescribed by the 1995 Notices Regulations) within three months of the date on which the higher amount was determined.

If such a notice is served and payment is duly made, the former tenant is entitled to apply for an overriding lease of the property (see 3.6). Former tenants should be careful, however, to make payments to the landlord only on receipt of a valid s 17 notice. In *MW Kellog v F Tobin* [1999] L & T Rev 513, it was held that a former tenant who pays arrears to the landlord as a result of the current tenant's default is not required to serve a s 17 notice on its assignee in order to recover such payments from the assignee under an express or implied indemnity in the assignment. It was also held that charges paid by the former tenant before service of a s 17 notice on him by the landlord were paid voluntarily and not recoverable, therefore, from the assignee under the terms of the indemnity in the assignment.

3.1.6 All leases: overriding leases

Sections 19 and 20 of the 1995 Act give a right to former tenants or guarantors who have paid arrears to take an overriding lease of the property, in order to give them a measure of control. This applies both to old and new tenancies.

The person claiming an overriding lease must make a written request to the landlord specifying the payment by virtue of which he claims to be entitled to the overriding lease, either at the time of making the payment under s 17 or within 12 months of making that payment (s 19(5)). The landlord must grant the overriding lease within a reasonable time of receiving the request and the claimant is responsible for the landlord's reasonable costs. The landlord is only obliged to grant one overriding lease in respect of any particular premises. The lease under which the arrears were paid is referred to in the 1995 Act as 'the relevant tenancy'.

The terms of the overriding lease are to be as follows:

- an overriding lease will be a tenancy of the reversion expectant on the relevant tenancy;

- it must be granted for a term equal to the remainder of the term of the relevant tenancy plus three days or the longest period (less than three days) that will not wholly displace the landlord's reversionary interest;

- it must contain the same covenants as the relevant tenancy (subject to modifications agreed between the parties) but there is no obligation on either party to reproduce any covenant of the relevant tenancy which is personal to the landlord or the tenant under that tenancy;

- where anything under the relevant tenancy operates by reference to the start date of that tenancy then the corresponding covenant of the overriding lease operates by reference to the same start date;
- there is no obligation to reproduce any covenant of the relevant tenancy which has become spent by the time the overriding lease is granted.

An overriding lease will be an old tenancy (no matter when it is granted) unless the original tenancy was a new tenancy. The overriding lease must state that it was granted pursuant to s 19 of the 1995 Act and whether or not it is a new tenancy.

3.1.7 New tenancies only: modification of s 19 of the Landlord and Tenant Act 1927

The 1995 Act inserts a new sub-s (1A) into s 19 of the 1927 Act. This allows the landlord to impose additional restrictions on the tenant's ability to assign.

These changes apply only to new tenancies. Residential leases are specifically excluded and s 19 of the 1927 Act does not, in any event, apply to agricultural leases, including the new farm business tenancies.

Section 19 of the 1927 Act provides that an agreement in a lease against assigning, underletting, charging or parting with possession without consent is deemed to be subject to a proviso that the consent will not be unreasonably withheld. It is important to note that the modification introduced by the 1995 Act applies only to assignment. Other forms of alienation will therefore still be governed by the original s 19.

Section 19(1A) provides:

(1A)Where the landlord and the tenant under a qualifying lease have entered into an agreement specifying for the purposes of this sub-section:

  (a) any circumstances in which the landlord may withhold his licence or consent to an assignment of the demised premises or any part of them; or

  (b) any conditions subject to which any such licence or consent may be granted,

then the landlord:

  (i) shall not be regarded as unreasonably withholding his licence or consent to any such assignment if he withholds it on the ground (and it is the case) that any such circumstances exist; and

(ii) if he gives any such licence or consent subject to any such conditions, shall not be regarded as giving it subject to unreasonable conditions,

and s 1 of the Landlord and Tenant Act 1988 (qualified duty to consent to assignment, etc) shall have effect subject to the provisions of this sub-section.

However, the 1995 Act goes on to provide that it cannot be left to the discretion of the landlord to determine whether or not the specified circumstances have arisen or the specified conditions have been complied with. Any agreement made between the landlord and the tenant for this purpose will revert to the scrutiny of the courts under s 19 of the 1927 Act to the extent that any circumstances or conditions specified in it are framed by reference to any matter falling to be determined by the landlord or by any other person unless, either that person's power to determine is required to be exercised reasonably, or the tenant is given an unrestricted right to have any such determination reviewed by an independent person whose identity is ascertainable by the terms of the agreement. In the latter case, the determination by the independent person must be conclusive as to the matter in question.

In other words, the circumstances or conditions must:

• be completely objective; or
• be applied by the landlord acting reasonably; or
• be applied by an independent third party whose appointment is provided for under the agreement.

In drafting assignment provisions, practitioners should bear in mind that, although tighter control over assignments may be desirable, this will have an adverse impact on valuation at rent review. Where appropriate, advice should be sought from a chartered surveyor on the valuation impact of new assignment provisions.

3.1.8 New tenancies only: transmission of covenants

Section 3 of the 1995 Act provides for the automatic transmission of the benefit and burden of all landlord and tenant covenants of a new tenancy, whether or not they have reference to the subject matter of the tenancy and whether they are express, implied or imposed by law. Accordingly, in relation to new tenancies, there is no need for the landlord to take up direct covenants from incoming tenants.

3.1.9 Anti-avoidance provisions

The 1995 Act contains draconian anti-avoidance provisions. Section 25(1) reads:

> Any agreement relating to a tenancy is void to the extent that:
>
> (a) it would apart from this section have effect to exclude, modify or otherwise frustrate the operation of any provision of this Act ...

Practitioners should familiarise themselves with the provisions of the Act and be careful to ensure that they do not inadvertently fall foul of the anti-avoidance provisions.

3.2   Contracts (Rights of Third Parties) Act 1999

3.2.1 Introduction

The doctrine of privity, which provides that a person who is not a party to a contract may not enforce it even though the contract or certain provisions thereof may have been made for that person's benefit, is amended by the Contracts (Rights of Third Parties) Act 1999 (the 1999 Act). The Act applies to contracts entered into at or after midnight on 11 May 2000, unless the parties to the contracts expressly provide to the contrary.

The Act creates a two limb test. Section 1(1) provides that a person who is not a party to a contract (a 'third party') may enforce a term of the contract if:

(a) the contract expressly provides that he may; or

(b) the terms purport to confer a benefit upon him.

The second limb is subject to the important proviso in s 1(2), whereby it will not apply 'if on a proper construction of the contract it appears that the parties did not intend the term to be enforceable by the third party'. In applying the proviso, it is not simply the wording of the contract that will be referred to, but the wider commercial context in which the contract operates. This potentially limits the number of third party claimants where the contract operates in an environment in which adequate remedies are available to the third party by suing along a chain.

The third party may be specifically named, but the Act also allows identification by class or description (s 1(3)). Thus, for example, a reference to 'all future tenants' of a building is sufficient identification of the class of third parties to whom rights are to be granted. Further, the person need not be in existence at the time of the contract, so that rights can conferred upon a company which is yet to be incorporated.

3.2.2 Third party consent to variations

Once a third party's right to enforcement has 'crystallised', the contracting parties cannot rescind or vary the contract so as to extinguish or alter the third party's entitlement without his consent (unless the contract provides otherwise). By s 2, the rights will crystallise if:

(a) the third party has communicated his assent to the term to the promisor;

(b) the promisor is aware that the third party has relied on the term; or

(c) the promisor can reasonably be expected to have foreseen that the third party would rely on the term and the third party has in fact relied on it.

Consent to variations can be dispensed with by the court if the third party cannot be traced or is mentally incapable of giving consent (s 2(4)). In such a situation, the court can order compensation to be paid to the third party (s 2(6)). More importantly, the contracting parties may provide in the original contract that the third party's consent is not required to the variation or set out the circumstances in which consent is required (s 2(3)).

3.2.3 Enforcement

The third party is to be treated as a 'party to the contract' and is given the same remedies as would be available if he were a contracting party. These will include not only damages, but injunctions, specific performance and other relief (s 1(5)). In an action by the third party, the promisor is able to rely on any defence or set off arising out of the contract and relevant to the term being enforced which would have been available to him had the claim been by the promisee (s 3). Again, this can be varied by the express terms of the contract. The promisor is also protected from double liability (s 5).

3.2.4 Enforcement of covenants between tenants

The Act *may* make it possible to enforce contracts between tenants (such as 'keep open' covenants in a shopping centre), or between tenants and adjoining owners or occupiers (such as covenants not to cause a nuisance or annoyance to 'the landlord or to any owner or occupier of any adjoining premises'). The question will often be whether or not such covenants are intended to 'confer a benefit'.

3.2.5 Enforcement of covenants by and against the superior landlord

The Act may affect the enforcement of covenants between superior landlords and sub-tenants. Usually, the sub-tenant is required to enter into a direct covenant with the superior landlord to observe the covenants in the sub-tenancy. Where this has not been done, but the sub-tenancy is drafted expressly to give the superior landlord direct rights of enforcement, then clearly the first limb (s 1(1)(a)) will have been satisfied. As for sub-tenancies which contain no express rights of enforcement, the covenants will have to 'confer a benefit' on the superior landlord if he is to be able to enforce them (s 1(1)(b)). The covenants most likely to arise are of two types:

(a) a covenant which gives the superior landlord rights to enter and to effect repairs at the sub-tenant's expense;

(b) a covenant which prohibits alienation by the sub-tenant without the consent of the superior landlord.

The preliminary issue will be whether these clauses 'confer a benefit' on the superior landlord or whether they are merely promises 'of benefit to' the superior landlord. It must also be then determined whether on 'a proper construction of the lease' it 'appears that the parties did not intend the term to be enforceable by the third party'.

Similarly, it is possible that a sub-tenant might have direct recourse against a superior landlord, perhaps for breach of covenant to provide a particular service. Superior landlords may wish to negate any presumption by express wording.

3.2.6 Exclusion of the 1999 Act

It is open to the contracting parties to state expressly that they do not want other persons to have a right to enforce any part of the contract. The parties may choose to exclude the Act from the lease unless there is, in a particular case, a special reason not to do so. In such a situation, it is suggested that an express clause is included, stating clearly the persons who are to have the benefit of any of the relevant terms and the basis and extent to which they are to have such benefit.

4 Statutory Renewal: Pt II of the Landlord and Tenant Act 1954

4.1 Introduction

A sound knowledge and understanding of the statutory provisions governing the renewal of business leases is essential for anyone involved in drafting commercial leases. A brief outline of some of the relevant principles is given here, but for a more detailed overview of these areas, see Aldridge, T, *Letting Business Premises*, 7th edn, 1996, FT Law & Tax.

Major changes have taken place in the context of lease renewals since the introduction of the Civil Procedure Rules (CPR), which came into effect in England and Wales on 26 April 1999. The CPR are intended to streamline litigation, and to make it easier for individuals to bring proceedings. A major feature is the allocation of cases to one of three tracks – small claims (for claims below £5,000 in value), fast track (for claims up to £15,000), or multi-track (for all other claims).

The 'overriding objective' of the CPR is to enable the court to deal with cases justly by, so far as practicable:

- ensuring that the parties are on an equal footing;
- saving expense;
- dealing with cases in ways which are proportionate to the amount of money involved, their importance, the complexity of the issues and the relative financial position of each party;
- ensuring that they are dealt with expeditiously and fairly; and
- allotting to them an appropriate share of the court's resources whilst taking into account the need to allot resources to other cases.

The court has a duty to give effect to the overriding objective and the parties themselves have a duty to help in furthering it. As a corollary to this, the court has an obligation to encourage, and the parties are expected independently to explore, the possibility of settlement at all stages of the proceedings.

The court also has an obligation actively to manage its cases. This means that it will no longer be left to the parties to determine the pace at which they pursue proceedings. Before 26 April 1999, it was not uncommon for practitioners involved in lease renewals to issue proceedings and then leave the matter, for months or even years, while the parties supposedly negotiated. Now, once proceedings have been started, the active case management powers of the court mean that neither party will be able to stall progress and that the procedural steps must be followed within the timetable set by the court.

The intention of the Civil Procedure Rules Committee was to carry out a separate reform of the Rules as they relate to landlord and tenant cases. In July 2000, the Lord Chancellor's department published a consultation paper entitled 'Access to Justice. Housing and Land: Proposed New Procedures'. It is proposed that all claims made under the 1954 Act will begin in the county court. This book focuses on county court procedure, therefore, and the procedure for making claims in the High Court is not dealt with.

Initially, there was considerable confusion among practitioners following the introduction of the CPR. The correct procedure to be used was by no means clear. Readers should note that:

- the procedure is regulated by Pt 8, Practice Direction 8B and specified provisions of the County Court Rules, which now appear in the Schedule to the CPR;

- Practice Direction 8B requires that the relevant claim form is Form N397, but practitioners and county court offices will often assume that a Pt 8 Claim Form is needed. Indeed, some county court offices have requested a Pt 8 Claim Form completed in accordance with the content of Form N397. CPR 3.10 provides that:

    ... where there has been an error of procedure such as a failure to comply with a rule or practice direction (a) the error does not invalidate any step taken in the proceedings unless the court so orders; and (b) the court may make an order to remedy the error.

The court should not, therefore, refuse to issue the claim because it is in the wrong form.

4.2 Application of the 1954 Act

The 1954 Act governs:

> ... any tenancy where the property comprised in the tenancy is, or includes premises which are, occupied by the tenant and are so occupied for the purposes of a business carried on by him or for those and other purposes [s 23].

4.2.1 'Any tenancy'

(a) A tenancy may be either periodic or for a fixed term. The term 'tenancy' in this context also includes:

- a sub-tenancy, whether lawful or unlawful (*D'Silva v Lister House Developments Ltd* [1971] Ch 17);

- an equitable tenancy;

- a tenancy by estoppel (*Bell v General Accident Fire and Life Assurance Corporation Ltd* [1998] 17 EG 144);

but *not*:

- a tenancy by will, whether arising by implication of law or expressly (*Wheeler v Mercer* [1957] AC 416; *Hagee Ltd v AB Erikson and Larson* [1976] QB 209; *Cardiothoracic Institute v Shrewdcrest Ltd* [1976] 3 All ER 633. See also *Javid v Acquil* [1991] 1 All ER 243).

(b) The following are excluded from the Act:

- a tenancy which is regulated under the Rent Act 1977 (s 24(3), Rent Act 1977) or an assured tenancy under the Housing Act 1988 (s 1 and Sched 1, para 4 of the Housing Act 1988) or a secure tenancy protected by the Housing Act 1985 (Sched 1, para 11 of the Housing Act 1985);

- tenancies of agricultural holdings and farm business tenancies (s 43(1)(a));

- mining leases (s 43(1)(b));

- service tenancies (s 43(2));

- a tenancy granted for a term certain of six months or less unless:
  - it contains a provision enabling it to be extended beyond that period; or
  - the tenant and any predecessor in the same business have been in occupation for a period which exceeds 12 months (s 43(3));

- a tenancy for a term of years certain in respect of which the parties have agreed to exclude the Act, provided the court approves such agreement before the tenancy was granted (s 38(4)). See 4.1.3;

- a tenancy where the user is in breach of a general prohibition on business use (s 23(4));

- tenancies of premises licensed to sell alcohol, not including hotels and restaurants and other premises where the sale of alcohol is not the main use of the premises, which were granted before 11 July 1989 (s 43(1)(d)). Tenancies of premises licensed to sell alcohol granted on or after 11 July 1989 do fall within the Act (s 1(1) of the Landlord and Tenant (Licensed Premises Act 1990).

4.2.2 Occupation

The tenant must remain in occupation if he is to enjoy the protection afforded by the 1954 Act. The point was clearly made by the Court of Appeal, in *Esselte AB v Pearl Assurance* [1997] 1 WLR 891, that the statutory code will apply only where the conditions contained in s 23 are satisfied at the time the contractual term ends. Thus, a fixed term will end by effluxion of time if, at the expiration of the term, the tenant has ceased to occupy the premises for the purposes of a business. Similarly, the landlord is able to serve an effective common law notice to quite on a non-occupying periodic tenant.

Usually, there will be no difficulty in determining whether or not the tenant is in occupation, but problems may arise where the tenant is allowing others to carry out some activity, business or otherwise, on the premises. In *Graysim Holdings Ltd v P and O Property Holdings Ltd* [1996] AC 329, the House of Lords held that the question is one of fact and degree. The premises comprised a market, the individual units of which had been sub-let by the tenant, who retained occupation only of the common parts and service rooms in the market hall. It was held that, on the facts of the case, this was insufficient to amount to business occupation on the tenant's part of either the common parts or the whole property. Thus, the only business user was that of the sub-tenants. As Lord Nicholls observed (p 343): '... intermediate landlords, not themselves in occupation are not within the class of persons the Act was seeking to protect.' It should be noted, however, that a tenant who has sub-let premises may still have retained such a degree of control over the use of the premises that he can be said to be 'occupying' them himself for the purposes of his business. See, for example, *Lee Verhulst (Investments) Ltd v Harwood Trust* [1973] 1 QB 204.

If the tenant chooses no longer to occupy the premises the protection of Pt II will be lost if that absence is sufficient to break 'the thread of continuity' (see *Aspinall Finance Ltd v Viscount Chelsea* [1989] 09 EG 77; *Demetriou v Poolaction Ltd* [1991] 1 EGLR 100). If, however, the absence is caused by circumstances beyond the tenant's control, occupation will not be deemed to have been relinquished by the tenant's absence provided that he had a realisable intention to return (see *I and H Caplan Ltd v Caplan (No 2)* [1963] 1 WLR 1247, in which the tenant moved out for seven months pending resolution of 1954 Act proceedings); *Morrison Holdings Ltd v Manders Property (Wolverhampton) Ltd* [1976] 1 WLR 533 (in which the tenants moved out following a fire in an adjoining property). Seasonal occupation has also been held to be continuous for the purposes of the Act (*Teasdale v Walker* [1958] 3 All ER 307, CA).

Sections 41 and 42 of the 1954 Act cover those situations where the tenancy is held on trust, and where the tenancy is held by a company within a group of companies.

4.2.3 'For the purposes of a business'

The tenant must occupy some part of the premises and the occupation must be at least partly for business purposes. Business is defined as including a trade profession or employment and any activity carried on by a body of persons (s 23(2)). The Act distinguishes, therefore, between a tenant who is an individual and a tenant which is a body of persons. For an individual to be a business tenant, he must be carrying out an activity which can be classed as a trade, profession or employment. Where the tenant is a body of persons, it appears that any activity will count as business purposes. Thus, the activity of a tennis club has been held to be a business purpose within the 1954 Act (*Addiscombe Garden Estates Ltd v Crabbe* [1958] 1 QB 513).

4.3   Effect of the 1954 Act

Where the tenancy is protected by this part of the 1954 Act, termination of the letting can occur only in certain ways:

• by forfeiture of the present or a superior lease;

• by surrender;

• by notice to quit given by the tenant where there is a periodic tenancy or a tenancy for a term certain subject to a clause permitting the tenant to break the term;

• by the tenant giving notice, at least three months before the contractual term date (that is, expiry of the fixed term), that he does not want the tenancy to continue (s 27(1));

- by the tenant holding under a fixed term serving not less than three months' written notice expiring on the date the tenancy would have expired by effluxion of time or on a quarter day thereafter (s 27(2));
- by service of a landlord's s 25 notice; or
- by service of a tenant's s 26 request.

It should be noted that the tenant cannot give a notice to quit nor surrender the tenancy before he has been in occupation for one month. Further, an agreement to surrender is void under s 38(1) unless approved by the court pursuant to s 38(4).

Otherwise, by virtue of s 24, a tenancy governed by the 1954 Act will automatically continue beyond the original agreed term on the same terms, save for those inconsistent with such a statutory continuation. As regards pre-1996 leases, the liability of the original tenant does not run into the continuation period unless there is a covenant to the contrary (*City of London Corporation v Fell* [1994] 1 AC 458, HL). Post-1996 leases no longer support original tenant liability by virtue of the Landlord and Tenant (Covenants) Act 1995.

4.4   Avoidance

A landlord may wish to avoid the Act, and whether the tenant co-operates is a matter for negotiation. The main methods of avoidance are:

- by granting a licence to the occupier. For a discussion of the distinction between a lease and a licence in the light of the leading case of *Street v Mountford* [1985] AC 809 HL, see Colbey, R, *Residential Tenancies,* 4th edn, 2001, London: Cavendish Publishing. It was pointed out in *Dresden Estates Ltd v Collinson* [1987] 1 EGLR 45, by Glidewell LJ, that 'the attributes of residential premises and business premises are often quite different' and that 'the indicia, which may make it more apparent in the case of a residential occupier that he is indeed a tenant, may be less applicable or be less likely to have that effect in the case of some business tenancies'. Nonetheless, save in exceptional situations, where the occupier has exclusive possession, there will be a lease no matter what the agreement is labelled. Unless the occupier genuinely has no exclusive possession (for example, where a supermarket grants a 'concession' to a newsagent to operate in a part of the store and reserves the right to move the newsagent to a different area), the safest approach is not to attempt to create a licence;
- by creating a tenancy at will, as in *Hagee (London) Ltd v Erikson (AB) and Larson* [1976] QB 209. This arises where a tenant occupies land

as a tenant with the landlord's consent on the basis that either party can bring the tenancy to an end at any time. The danger for the landlord is that regular payments of rent may show that the real intention was to create a periodic tenancy which would be protected by the 1954 Act. Perhaps the best approach is to have a written document stating that a tenancy at will is created and providing for rent to accrue on a daily basis and to be payable at any time when demanded (see Precedent 8.1). A tenancy at will is especially useful as a stopgap measure to enable the tenant to enter into possession pending the court's approval being obtained to a fixed term tenancy excluded from the Act's protection. It can also be used as a means of documenting the occupancy arrangements where the tenant is holding over following the expiry of an excluded lease and pending completion of a new lease. However, the deployment of the express tenancy at will as a method of avoiding the protection afforded to tenants by the 1954 Act has two drawbacks: it confers neither a secure period of occupation for the tenant, nor a secure period of income for the landlord;

- a fixed term tenancy not exceeding six months, provided that there is no term allowing for renewal beyond this period (s 43(3)). In any event, the tenant and any business predecessor must not have together been in occupation for more than 12 months. Obviously, this method is only useful for a temporary short term letting. Because s 43(3) applies only to tenancies for a term certain, any kind of periodic tenancy will qualify for the protection of the Act from its inception, regardless of the length of time during which the tenant or the tenant's predecessors have been in occupation. In *Cricket v Shaftesbury plc* (1999) 28 EG 127, it was held that a tenancy which, on its expiry, falls outside the Act by virtue of s 43(3), cannot be retrospectively revived and brought within the Act by a subsequent period of occupation as a licensee, a trespasser or a tenant at will. It appears that the restriction applies at the time the tenancy is granted (rather than when it comes to an end), but the point has never been judicially decided. If the landlord grants the tenant a periodic tenancy at the end of the second tenancy, the new tenancy will be protected from the outset. It is important, therefore, that landlords take care over the arrangements under which tenants remain in possession at the end of excluded short leases.

Where the tenant has not been in occupation for a period exceeding 12 months, but is seeking to rely on the occupation of a predecessor, it is not clear whether the predecessor has to have been a tenant or may, for example, have been a freeholder, a tenant at will or a licensee;

- a fixed term tenancy (see *Nicholls v Kinsey* [1994] 2 WLR 622) where the parties agree that the 1954 Act will not apply and the court, on a joint application being made, authorises this agreement before the tenancy is created (s 38(4) and see *Essexcrest Ltd v Evenlex Ltd* [1988] 1 EG 56). This is usually the best method of avoiding the Act. Approval in most cases is readily obtained, although the parties should be independently advised (see Precedents in 8.2). Agreements which purport to preclude the tenant from renewing a business lease are void where the court's approval has not been obtained (s 38(1)).

In *Receiver for the Metropolitan Police District v Palacegate Properties Ltd* [2000] 3 All ER 663, the Court of Appeal held that the purpose of the legislation permitting the exclusion of a lease was to enable the court to be satisfied that the prospective tenant understood that it would not have the protection of the 1954 Act. The terms of the actual lease had to be substantially similar to the agreed form of draft lease submitted when applying for the order. The court considered that material changes, such as an alteration in the length of the lease or the area demised, might mean that the exclusion order was rendered invalid. However, the court held that the particular changes (that, according to the draft lease submitted to the court, the rent was to be paid annually in arrear whereas the parties had agreed all along that the rent would be payable quarterly in advance) would not affect the tenant's understanding that he was giving up protection of the 1954 Act.

Readers should note that there are moves afoot to abolish this procedure. See Raynsford, N, 'Better for both parties' (2000) EG, 25 November.

4.5 Procedure

(See also 2.2, and the Precedents in 9.3 and explanatory notes thereto.)

4.5.1 The 'competent landlord'

The tenant who may acquire the right to a renewal of its tenancy will want to negotiate the new tenancy with the landlord who has a substantial interest in the property. If the tenant's immediate landlord is the freeholder, this will present no problem. However, if the tenant is a sub-tenant, it is possible that the landlord may hold a term which is only a few days longer than the tenant's own.

The 1954 Act therefore provides a mechanism for identifying one landlord with whom the tenant should deal. This landlord is known as the competent landlord. Only a competent landlord is entitled to serve a s 25 notice on the tenant. If the tenant wishes to apply for a new tenancy, its request under s 26 should be served on the competent landlord. The competent landlord will not always be the tenant's immediate landlord.

Section 44(1) provides that the competent landlord will be either:

(a) the owner of the fee simple; or

(b) the landlord lowest in the chain of tenancies who has a tenancy which will not come to an end within 14 months by effluxion of time, and no notice has been given which will end the tenancy within 14 months.

In other words, a landlord whose own lease is coming to an end within 14 months drops out of the picture.

In order that the steps required by the renewal process are taken by the correct person at the correct time, both parties must be able to identify each other and to ascertain the nature and extent of their respective interests. This will be particularly important where a sub-letting has occurred. By s 40, either party may serve a notice on the other so as to obtain the necessary information. It should be noted, however, that a s 40 notice cannot be served by or on a tenant more than two years before the date on which the lease is due to expire or can be brought to an end by a landlord's notice to quit. See 9.3.1 and 9.3.2.

If there has been a recent assignment, it is important to make sure that the registration of that assignment been completed (if, of course, the lease is registrable). If it has not, then it is generally the legal owner (whether of the reversion or lease term interest) who must serve any notice or commence any proceedings and be the party upon whom such a notice or proceedings are served (*Brown and Root Technology Ltd v Sun Alliance and London Assurance Co Ltd* (1997) 75 P&CR 223).

4.5.2 Landlord's notice of termination

The landlord should serve a notice on the tenant under s 25 in a prescribed form or a form substantially to like effect. Where the landlord has not used the prescribed form or a form substantially to like effect, the notice will be invalid, irrespective of whether the tenant was or was not actually misled (*Sun Alliance and London Assurance Ltd v Hayman* [1975] 1 WLR 177; *Sabella Ltd v Montgomery and Others* [1998] 09 EG 153). However, a notice which mistakenly specifies a determination date will be valid if the reasonable recipient, with knowledge of the terms of the lease, is left in no doubt (*Mannai Investment Co Ltd v Eagle Star Life Assurance Co Ltd* [1997] AC 749).

Failure to comply with any or all of the following requirements will invalidate the notice, but the landlord who discovers an error or omission may serve a new and valid notice (*Smith v Draper* (1990) 60 P&CR 252).

The s 25 notice should:

• specify the date on which the landlord wishes the tenancy to end, such date being not more than 12 nor less than six months after the service of the notice and not earlier than the contractual term date or the date on which the landlord could have terminated by notice to quit in the case of a periodic tenancy (s 25(2) and (3));

• require the tenant, within two months of service, to notify the landlord in writing whether or not he is willing to give up possession on the date specified above (s 25(5));

• state whether the landlord would oppose an application to the court for the grant of a new tenancy and, if so, on which of the seven grounds set out in s 30 he would do so (s 25(6); see Precedent 8.3.1).

4.5.3 Action by tenant on receipt of landlord's notice

If the tenant wishes to apply for a new tenancy he must, within two months of the landlord's notice, serve written notice that he is unwilling to give up possession. (There is no prescribed form for this counter-notice, but see below, 9.3.4.) Failure to comply with these strict time limits will mean that the tenant's right to seek a new tenancy is lost unless the landlord is estopped by having made a representation that the tenant will be granted a new tenancy which the tenant has relied on to its detriment (*JT Developments Ltd v Quinn* [1991] 2 EGLR 257).

If no agreement is reached following service of the tenant's counter-notice, the tenant may apply to court for a new tenancy not less than two, nor more than four months after the giving of the landlord's s 25 notice (s 29(3)).

4.5.4 Tenant's request for a new tenancy

Instead of waiting for the landlord to serve a s 25 notice, the tenant can take the initiative and seek a new tenancy by serving a s 26 notice. The tenant may not want the present tenancy to come to an end if rents have risen since the rent was fixed or last reviewed, but there can be an advantage to the tenant in serving a s 26 request for a tenancy 12 months hence, where the landlord has delayed and is about to serve a s 25 notice with a termination date less than 12 months hence. This tactical manoeuvre will delay the commencement of a new tenancy with its revised rent. The tenant will wish to achieve the opposite effect by serving a s 26 request to come into effect as soon as possible where the open market rent is less than the current rent.

Unlike the s 25 procedure, the s 26 route is only available where the tenancy was granted for a term certain of more than one year, or for a term of more than one year and then from year to year (s 26(1)). Thus, a yearly tenant, for example, must wait until the landlord has served notice on him before applying for a new tenancy.

A s 26 request can be served whether the contractual fixed term is still subsisting or has been extended by s 24. It must be in the form prescribed by the Act (see Precedent 9.3.5). The request must specify:

- the date for the commencement of the new tenancy, being not more than 12, nor less than six months after the making of the request, and not earlier than the date on which the existing tenancy would have expired by effluxion of time or could be brought to an end by notice to quit given by the tenant (s 26(2));
- the tenant's proposals for the new tenancy, that is, as to:
  - the property to be comprised in the new tenancy (being either the whole or part of the property comprised in the current tenancy);
  - the rent payable under the new tenancy; and
  - the other terms of the new tenancy.

Where the tenant exercises a break clause in a fixed term tenancy, the contractual term ends, and so does any statutory protection. The tenant cannot then serve a request for a new lease and there is no need for the landlord to serve a termination notice (_Garston v Scottish Widows Fund_ [1998] 3 All ER 596, in which the Court of Appeal held that it was not the purpose of s 26 to allow the tenant to choose to terminate a tenancy prematurely and then apply for a new tenancy on more favourable terms.)

Service of notices is as provided by s 23 of the 1927 Act (s 66(4) of the 1954 Act, and see 8.2.2). The time limits are strict (see the summary in 2.2), and once the landlord has served a s 25 notice, the tenant cannot serve a s 26 request, and vice versa (s 26(4)). If the tenant serves a request but does not apply to the court in time, he cannot start again by serving another, and the tenancy will end on the date for commencement of the new term stated in the request (_Polyviou v Seeley_ [1980] 1 WLR 55).

4.5.5 Action by the landlord on receipt of the tenant's request

A landlord who wishes to oppose any application by the tenant to court for a new tenancy must, within two months of the tenant's request, serve a counter-notice (for which there is no prescribed form, but see Precedent 9.3.6), stating that he will oppose such an application, and on which statutory ground(s) he will do so.

4.5.6 PACT

As an alternative to the courts, the terms of a new business tenancy can be determined by arbitration or by an independent expert following the implementation of PACT (Professional Arbitration on Court Terms), a voluntary scheme which has been developed jointly by the Law Society and Royal Institute of Chartered Surveyors with the support of the Incorporated Society of Valuers and Auctioneers.

The scheme applies to unopposed lease renewals under the 1954 Act. The tenant serves its s 26 request or counter-notice to the landlord's s 25 notice and then applies to the court within the time limits imposed by the 1954 Act. Any grounds of opposition will be dealt with by the court. The parties then record by way of consent order the terms upon which they are agreed (if any), and outstanding matters are then referred to arbitration or an independent expert who is required to apply the statutory criteria in reaching the award on the terms of the new tenancy. Once the arbitration or expert determination has taken place, either party may (under the terms of the consent order) go back to the court if necessary for an order under s 29 for a new tenancy on the terms which have been determined. The tenant's right, under s 36(2), to elect not to take up the tenancy, is preserved.

Full details of the scheme, including Guidance Notes, an application form for the appointment of an expert or arbitrator, and model consent orders can be found on the RICS website: www.RICS.org.uk.

4.5.7 The court application

The tenant must apply to court for a new tenancy not less than two, nor more than four, months after service of the landlord's s 25 notice or the tenant's request under s 26 (s 29(3)). Unless the landlord agrees, an application cannot be made outside of these dates (*Kammin's Ballrooms Co Ltd v Zenith Investments (Torquay) Ltd* [1971] AC 850).

The tenant's application can be made either to the county court or the High Court. Since 1991, the county court has had an unlimited jurisdiction to determine applications under the 1954 Act and any former jurisdictional limitations based on rateable values are no longer relevant. Thus, although the High Court remains an option for the tenant, most lease renewals are dealt with by the county court.

Where, as is usually the case, the terms of a new tenancy are agreed prior to there being a court hearing, the agreement can either be embodied in a court order (for the county court's powers to make such an order on the day fixed for the hearing see CCR Ord 43, r 15(1)) or, more simply, the tenant can withdraw the application on the agreed terms (see CCR Ord 18, r 1 and the Precedents in 9.3.9 and 9.3.10 and accompanying notes). If the parties agree a new term, the current tenancy will not continue beyond the agreed date of commencement of the new term and Pt II will then cease to apply to the former term (s 28).

Pre-action conduct

At present, pre-action protocols exist only in relation to medical negligence and personal injury cases. Even where pre-action protocols do not apply, however, the parties are expected to adhere to their philosophy. Before proceedings are commenced, therefore, a claimant will be required to have done much of its case preparation and explored the possibility of settlement (CPR, Practice Direction: Protocols, para 4). The requirement to exchange information is particularly appropriate in lease renewal claims because the parties are likely to have their intentions firmly settled at an early stage. The landlord will have specified his ground of opposition (if any) to a new lease in his s 25 notice or in his counter-notice to the tenant's s 26 request and, by the time any counter-notice has been served, should be in a position to provide the tenant with such information he has in support of that ground. For example, if the landlord proposes to redevelop and has applied for, or obtained, planning permission, the relevant documents should be sent to the tenant.

Whether or not the landlord opposes the new tenancy, there will usually be some dispute as to the rent to be paid, should the tenant be granted a new tenancy. Thus, as soon as it is apparent that the tenant will be pursuing a claim for a new tenancy (that is, as soon as a counter-notice has been served) the parties should be taking steps to agree upon an expert who will be acceptable to both parties.

In proceedings under the 1954 Act, the courts have traditionally looked to parties to bear their own costs. The CPR, however, give the courts new powers, when awarding costs, to take account of the parties' pre-action conduct.

The claim form

The CPR have substantially affected the court applications required by
Part II of the Landlord and Tenant Act 1954 regarding lease renewal
cases. In both the county court and the High Court, proceedings are
commenced by claim form. Strictly, writs, summons and originating
applications have no part to play in the new system.

Service must take place within two months of the issue of the claim
form (CCR Ord 43, r 6(3)). It can be carried out either by the court
or by the claimant personally. If served by the court, the court must
notify the claimant when service has occurred. If service is by the
claimant, the claimant must file a certificate of service within seven days
of service taking place (CPR, r 6.10). The permitted methods of service
include personal service, first class post, leaving the document at the
address for service of the party, through a document exchange or by
fax or other means of electronic communication.

Stay pending negotiations

When a defendant files a defence, the court may serve an allocation
questionnaire on each party. If it does so, either party may make a written
request for the proceedings to be stayed while the parties try to settle
the case. Where all parties request a stay, or the court of its own initiative
considers that such a stay would be appropriate, the court will direct
that the proceedings be stayed for one month. The court may extend
the stay until such date or for such period as it considers appropriate
(CPR 26.4).

Where no allocation questionnaire is sent out, but the parties wish
to have the proceedings stayed for the purpose of negotiations, they
should write to the court making a request for such a stay and refer to
CPR 26.4. If more than one month is required, reasons should be given.

Where the proceedings are stayed, the tenant must tell the court
that the claim has been settled or the parties must write to the court
requesting a further extension of time, or an allocation questionnaire
should be filed at court (CPR 26.4(4)). If the tenant does not do so by
the end of the period of the stay, the court will give such directions as
to the management of the case as it considers appropriate (CPR 26.4(5)).

Case management

In the past, it was often the case that, on a lease renewal, the court
application was made and then the lease terms were agreed in negotiations
without further recourse to the court. Hearings to settle the lease terms

were rare. Under the previous procedure, no date for a hearing was fixed, as the application was really only made to protect the statutory right of the tenant to renew. Under the new procedure, however, the court is obliged actively to manage cases and take this responsibility from the parties.

Active case management includes:

(a) encouraging the parties to co-operate with each other in the conduct of the proceedings;

(b) identifying the issues at an early stage;

(c) deciding promptly which issues need full investigation and trial and accordingly disposing summarily of the others;

(d) deciding the order in which issues are to be resolved;

(e) encouraging the parties to use an alternative dispute resolution procedure if the court considers that appropriate and facilitating the use of such procedure;

(f) helping the parties to settle the whole or part of the case;

(g) fixing timetables or otherwise controlling the progress of the case;

(h) considering whether the likely benefits of taking a particular step justify the cost of taking it;

(i) dealing with as many aspects of the case as it can on the same occasion;

(j) dealing with the case without the parties needing to attend at court;

(k) making use of technology; and

(l) giving directions to ensure that the trial of a case proceeds quickly and efficiently; when the court issues the claim it should also fix the date for hearing.

The first hearing

In the county court, the court will fix a return day which, unless it otherwise directs, shall be the day fixed for the case management hearing of the proceedings (CCR Ord 43, r 2(1)). The case management hearing takes place before the district judge. If on the day fixed for the hearing the district judge is satisfied that:

• the parties have agreed on the subject, period and terms of the new tenancy;

• the owner of any reversionary interest in the property consents thereto; and

• there are no other persons with interests in the property who are likely to be affected, the district judge has the power to make an order giving effect to the agreement (CCR Ord 43, r15).

Otherwise, directions will be made for the matter ultimately to be tried. The directions will include decisions about whether or not to issue allocation questionnaires and the allocation of the case to a track, or directions to enable the case to be allocated. Renewal cases will fall into the latter two categories. Where the only matter in dispute is the rent, the fast track will probably be appropriate, particularly where the court also orders a report from a single joint expert (see above, Pre-action conduct). The appropriate track in other cases will obviously depend very much on the circumstances of the case. The consultation paper proposes that, at this stage, it will be possible to apply to the court for proceedings to be stayed for agreed time periods in which to negotiate.

Preliminary issues

Where the tenant's application contains an alternative claim to that for a new tenancy (for example, challenging the validity of a s 25 notice), or the landlord denies the tenant's right to apply for a new tenancy, it will normally be appropriate for that issue to be determined as a preliminary issue. If the landlord disputes the application for a new tenancy on one of the grounds set out in s 30 of the 1954 Act, it is likely that disclosure will be appropriate. It is also likely that the district judge will order that this question be determined as a preliminary issue.

If it is agreed that a new tenancy should be granted, but the terms are in dispute, disclosure will probably not be necessary, but it will be necessary to make an order for a draft lease to be submitted (usually) by the landlord to the tenant within a certain period of time and for the tenant to make his amendments to the draft within so many days thereafter.

Expert evidence

Expert evidence is usually required, for example, as to comparables or redevelopment. The court may direct that a report by a single joint expert should be ordered (CPR 35.7), but if the parties cannot agree a joint report, the court generally authorises separate experts provided that the issues are sufficiently complex.

The direction should provide for any expert evidence as to rent not to be prepared until after the other terms have been agreed or determined. This follows from the requirement of s 34(1) of the 1954 Act that the rent payable shall be such sum at which 'having regard to the terms of the tenancy (other than those relating to rent) the holding might reasonably be expected to be let in the open market'. If the parties cannot agree on the other terms first, it may be necessary to come back to court for further directions.

Other matters

Other matters that may need to be dealt with are:

- any application by the landlord for an interim rent;
- the joinder of other persons such as superior or mesne landlords who may be affected by any order of the court.

Answer

The landlord is not required to serve an acknowledgment of service, but must file an answer (CCR Ord 43, r 2(1)): see Precedent 9.3.8). The date upon which the answer must be served is not given but, given that the first hearing will be a case management conference, the answer should be served in advance so that the appropriate directions can be given and the case advanced.

Interim rent

As the new tenancy will not commence until three months after the application has been determined by the court (s 64), the landlord should apply to the court for an interim rent to be fixed once the s 25 notice or s 26 request has been served. This will operate from the date of termination or commencement stated in the s 25 notice or s 26 request, or from the commencement of interim rent proceedings if later (s 24A), and it will continue until the current tenancy comes to an end. In making the determination, the court shall have regard to the rent payable under the terms of the tenancy, but otherwise the court should determine the rent as it would under s 34(1) and (2) as if a new periodic yearly tenancy were to be granted of the whole premises (that is, not just the holding).

An interim rent application may be made by claim form using the Pt 8 procedure (PD 8B, para B(1)(3)(b) and B.8(3)), or it may arise in the course of the tenant's renewal proceedings, in which case it will be made in the landlord's answer (see below, 9.3.8). The landlord can, when drafting the lease, avoid the need for such an application by providing that there shall be a rent review near to the end of the original term (often one day prior to that date), but this will not always be accepted by tenants!

Discontinuance

A claimant may discontinue proceedings in the High Court or the county court under CPR Pt 38. The process involves the tenant filing a notice of discontinuance and serving a copy of it on every party (CPR, r 38.3). The discontinuance 'takes effect on the date when notice of discontinuance is served' on the defendant under CPR, r 38.3 (see CPR, r 38.5). The defendant may apply within 28 days to have the notice of discontinuance set aside (CPR, r 38.4), but subject to that right 'the proceedings are brought to an end as against him on that date'. In a lease renewal claim, this means that the tenancy will come to an end three months after that date (s 64 of the 1954 Act).

There are certain cases where permission to discontinue is required, for example, where the court has granted an interim injunction, but they are unlikely to apply in lease renewal claims (38.2).

Pre-discontinuation costs will normally be payable by the tenant (CPR, r 38.6).

4.6   Grounds for possession

At the hearing by the court of the tenant's application for a new tenancy, the landlord may rely only on such of the s 30 grounds as have been specified in the statutory notice or in his reply to the tenant's request.

Of the seven grounds summarised below, (a) (b) (c) and (e) are discretionary:

(a) failure to repair;

(b) persistent delay in paying rent;

(c) substantial breaches of other tenancy obligations;

(d) provision of suitable alternative premises;

(e) the premises form part of a property comprised in a superior tenancy and the aggregate rents reasonably obtainable on separate lettings would be substantially less than that reasonably obtainable on a letting of the property as a whole, and the landlord requires possession for that purpose;

(f) on termination of the current tenancy, the landlord intends to demolish or reconstruct the premises comprised in the holding or a substantial part of those premises, or to carry out substantial works of construction on the holding or part thereof and cannot reasonably do so without obtaining possession of the holding.

The landlord's intention

The intention is to be established at the date of the hearing (*Betty's Cafes v Phillips Furnishing Stores* [1959] AC 20). The existence of the landlord's intention is a question of fact and degree and must be assessed objectively. It must have 'moved out of the zone of contemplation – the sphere of the tentative, the provisional and the exploratory – and moved into the valley of decision' (*Cunliffe v Goodman* [1950] 2 KB 237, p 254).

It will be easier for the landlord to establish the requisite intention where the premises are 'old and worn out or are ripe for development, the proposed work is obviously desirable, plans and arrangements are well in hand, and the landlord has the means and ability to carry out the work'. The court will not be so readily satisfied, however, where 'the premises are comparatively new or the desirability of the project is open to doubt, when there are many difficulties still to be surmounted, such as the preparation and approval of plans or the obtaining of finance, or when the landlord has in the past fluctuated in his mind as to what to do with the premises' (*per* Denning LJ in *Reohorn v Barry Corporation* [1956] 2 All ER 742, p 744). It will assist the landlord if any necessary planning permission or building regulation consent has been obtained by the time of the hearing.

An intention to carry out the demolition and reconstruction need not be the primary purpose, and in *Fisher v Taylors Furnishing Stores Ltd* [1956] 2 All ER 78, the fact that the landlords intended to occupy the rebuilt premises themselves was held not to deprive them of their right to possession. The tenant has no recourse against a landlord who recovers possession and then changes his mind (*Reohorn v Barry Corporation* [1956] 2 All ER 742).

It must be the landlord who intends to demolish or reconstruct, but the work need not be done by the landlord; it may be done by the landlord's employees or agents or by building contractors, or even under a building lease by which the lessee is to do the rebuilding (*Gilmour Caterers Ltd v St Bartholomew's Hospital Governors* [1956] 1 QB 387; *Turner v Wandsworth LBC* [1994] 1 EGLR 134).

Demolition, reconstruction or substantial reconstruction

To reconstruct means to rebuild, involving substantial interference with the structure of the building (*Percy E Cadle and Co Ltd v Jacmarch Properties* [1957] 1 QB 323, conversion of three separate floors into one unit by putting in new staircases did not come within ground (f)); cf *Joel v Swaddle* [1957] 1 WLR 1094, conversion of a small shop with two storage rooms into part of a larger amusement arcade.

Work could not reasonably be done without obtaining possession

Where the landlord could carry out the proposed work with possession of part only, or by being given access to and other facilities over the premises then, if the tenant agrees, possession can be ordered on that basis and the landlord will not get possession of the whole premises. The landlord cannot use this ground where the right to enter to carry out the works has been reserved and legal possession (rather than physical possession) is not therefore needed (*Heath v Drown* [1973] AC 498 and *Price v Esso Petroleum Co Ltd* [1980] 255 EG 243) save perhaps where the works are so substantial that the tenant cannot afterwards operate the business permitted under the lease (*Leathwoods Ltd v Total Oil (Great Britain) Ltd* [1984] 270 EG 1083). See 6.3 for the drafting implications of *Heath v Drown*.

The need for possession for the purposes of ground (f) must be considered alongside s 31A (added by the Law of Property Act 1969), which provides that the court shall not hold that the landlord cannot reasonably carry out the works, etc, without obtaining permission if either:

- the tenant agrees to the inclusion in the new tenancy of terms giving the landlord access and other facilities for carrying out the intended work provided that this would be sufficient to enable the work to be carried out without possession being obtained and without interfering to a substantial extent or for a substantial time with the tenant's use of the premises for the purposes of his business (s 31A(1)(a)); or
- the tenant is willing to accept a tenancy of an economically separate part of the holding and either (a) above is satisfied in respect of that part or possession of the remainder of the holding would be reasonably sufficient to enable the landlord to carry out the intended work (s 31A(1)(b)). For this purpose, the court will not modify the landlord's plans or question whether the landlord's intentions are reasonable, provided that they are *bona fide* (*Decca Navigator Co Ltd v GLC* [1974] 1 WLR 748).

(g) On the termination of the current tenancy, the landlord intends to occupy the premises wholly or partly as his residence, or for the purposes of a business to be carried on by him or by a company which he controls.

As with ground (f), this intention must be shown to exist at the date of the hearing. In *Dolgellau Golf Club v Hett* [1998] 34 EG 87, the Court of Appeal underlined the point that whether a landlord can rely on ground (g) depends on the reasonable practicability of the landlord's intention to start a business. The probability of achieving its start or its likely success once established are irrelevant.

Ground (g) is unavailable where the landlord's interest was purchased or created within five years of the end of the tenancy. The current tenancy ends on the date of termination stated in the landlord's s 25 notice or the date of commencement of a new tenancy stated in the tenant's s 26 request. Where the landlord is delaying in order to rely on this ground, until he has been a landlord by purchase for five years, an astute tenant can serve a s 26 request and thereby obtain a new tenancy.

Where a landlord seeks to rely on ground (d), (e) or (f), but fails to establish the ground to the court's satisfaction, s 31(2) provides a further opportunity of obtaining possession where the ground can be satisfied at a later date.

4.7   New terms

This will often be the only issue between the parties who will serve notices and apply to court merely to protect their respective positions. The Act provides that the terms will be as agreed or:

- the tenancy will normally be of *the holding*, that is, that part of the premises currently occupied by the tenant for the purposes of a business (ss 23(3) and 32) unless:

  (a) the landlord has opposed the grant of a new tenancy on ground (f) and, in accordance with s 31A(1), the tenant has agreed to accept a tenancy of an economically separable part of the existing holding to enable the landlord to carry out proposed works, etc. In such a case, the order will necessarily be for a new tenancy of that separate part;

  (b) there are other premises comprised in the current tenancy as well as the holding and the landlord requires the tenant to take a new tenancy of the whole (s 32(2)). Thus, a tenant who intends to sub-let part, or the whole, of the premises should first be advised of the effect that this can have on renewal.

  By s 32(3), where the current tenancy includes rights enjoyed by the tenant in connection with the holding, those rights shall be included in the new tenancy unless the parties agree to the contrary. If the parties cannot agree, the court will determine which rights should be included (see, for example, *Re No 1 Albemarle Street W1* [1959] Ch 531);

- the court has a discretion to determine what it considers to be a reasonable *duration* in all the circumstances up to a maximum of 14 years (s 33), although a longer term can be agreed between the parties. The new tenancy can be a periodic tenancy or for a fixed term. The court's discretion is wide and it will take into account:

(a) the length of the original term;

(b) the length of time over which the tenant has held over under the current tenancy;

(c) the balance of hardship and relative bargaining positions (*Amika Motors Ltd v Colebrook Holdings Ltd* [1981] 259 EG 243);

(d) the landlord's future plans for the property. Thus, where the premises are ripe for future development, the court may be persuaded by the landlord to grant a short term or to order a new tenancy containing a break clause (see cases such as *Reohorn v Barry Corporation* [1956] 2 All ER 742, *Adams v Green* [1978] 247 EG 49 and *Amika Motors Ltd v Colebrook Holdings Ltd* [1981] 259 EG 243);

• by s 34(1), the *rent* fixed by the court will be the amount at which the holding might be expected to be let in the open market by a willing lessor having regard to the terms of the new lease but disregarding:

(a) the effect on rent attributable to occupation by the tenant (or a predecessor in title) of the holding;

(b) goodwill of the tenant's business;

(c) improvements made voluntarily by the tenant or during the past 21 years; and

(d) the benefit of any licence where the premises are licensed.

The effect of the 1995 Act on rent is to be taken into account.

The court can provide for the rent to be reviewed during the term even where there is no rent review clause in the current lease (s 34). This is standard practice in tenancies other than short tenancies, and the tendency has been to order review clauses which permit the rent to move upwards or downwards;

• in fixing *terms other than as to duration and rent*, the court must have regard to the terms of the current tenancy and to all relevant circumstances, including the operation of the Landlord and Tenant (Covenants) Act 1995 (s 35(1)). In *O'May v City of London Real Property Company* [1983] 2 AC 726, HL, it was held that the onus is on the party proposing a change in the original terms to show that it is fair and reasonable. Thus, the tenant should resist the imposition of new, more onerous terms such as changing the basis of repairing obligations so that the financial burden falls on the tenant. The tenant on a statutory renewal is, therefore, in a much stronger position than a new tenant negotiating the terms of a lease.

In *Wallis Fashion Group Limited v CGU Life Assurance Limited* [2000] 27 EG 145, it was held that, upon the statutory renewal of a pre-

1996 lease, the landlord cannot insist upon the inclusion of a term under which, upon assignment, the tenant must automatically enter into an authorised guarantee agreement (AGA: see 3.3.2). It appears that the most the landlord can hope for is a term under which the tenant must, if reasonably required to do so, enter into a pre-agreed form of AGA.

It remains to be seen whether a landlord can achieve stricter alienation provisions in the light of the 1995 Act.

4.8   Following the court's order

If the landlord opposes the application on one or more of the grounds specified in s 30(1) and establishes any of those grounds to the court's satisfaction, the court cannot order the grant of a new tenancy. The existing tenancy continues for three months after the proceedings have finally been disposed of (s 64).

If a new tenancy is ordered by the court, the landlord is bound to execute the new tenancy and the tenant is bound to accept it (s 36(1)). However, the tenant may apply, within 14 days, for the revocation of the order if he is unwilling to accept its terms (s 36(2)). The current tenancy will continue for such period as the parties agree or for as long as the court deems necessary to allow the landlord a reasonable opportunity for re-letting or otherwise disposing of the premises. Where no such application is made by the tenant, the new tenancy begins three months after the final determination of the proceedings.

4.9   Compensation

4.9.1 Compensation for disturbance

If the court is precluded from ordering a new tenancy solely because one or more of grounds (e), (f) or (g) above are established, the tenant is entitled to compensation under s 37. Section 37 will apply where:

- the tenant has applied for a new tenancy and the landlord has successfully opposed the claim on one or more of those grounds (but on no other ground); or
- the landlord has specified grounds (e), (f) or (g) in his notice and the tenant has applied for a new tenancy, but has since withdrawn the application; or
- the landlord has specified grounds (e), (f) or (g) in his notice and the tenant has not applied for a new tenancy.

Compensation will be the rateable value, or double this sum, where the tenant or his business predecessors have been in occupation for at least 14 years immediately preceding the termination of the current tenancy (Landlord and Tenant Act 1954 (Appropriate Multiplier) Order 1990 SI 1990/363). The 'termination of the current tenancy' is the date specified in the landlord's s 25 notice or the tenant's s 26 request, which may be different from the date the tenant quits the premises (*Sight and Sound Education Ltd v Books etc Ltd* [1999] 43 EG 161).

The usual provision in a lease that the tenant shall not be entitled to such compensation is effective where the period of business occupation will be less than five years 'immediately preceding the date on which the tenant ... is to quit'. The occupation of the tenant's predecessors is included for this purpose, provided that the same business has been carried on in the premises (s 38(2)). It is clear from *Bacchiocchi v Academic Agency Ltd* [1998] 2 All ER 241 that 'the date on which the tenant ... is to quit' is that on which the tenant will be legally required to give up possession to the landlord. It is not necessarily the date specified in the renewal documentation but may be, for example, three months following the final disposal of the proceedings.

It should be noted that the tenant's right to compensation arises on quitting the premises. It was held in *Webb v Sandown Sports Club* [2000] EGCS 13 that a tenant who had found new premises and moved his stock into them, had 'quit' the premises even though the landlord had peaceably re-entered them one month after the tenant's departure.

Alternative transitional provisions apply to business premises with a domestic element (*Busby v Co-operative Insurance Society Ltd* [1994] 6 EG 141). Where the tenancy was entered into before 1 April 1990 (or after that date pursuant to a contract before it) and the landlord's s 25 notice or s 26(6) counter-notice was given before 1 April 2000, the tenant may be able to elect for compensation at eight (or 16, if there has been at least 14 years' occupation) times the old rateable value on 31 March 1990 by giving notice to the landlord within two and four months of the s 25 notice or s 26 request (Sched 7, para 4 Local Government and Housing Act 1989).

4.9.2 Compensation for improvements

Compensation may also be available for the tenant's voluntary improvements, no matter what the ground for possession under the Landlord and Tenant Act 1927 (see 2.3).

5 Rent Review

5.1 Purpose

Rent review is a very complex area of law and it has been said that a decision interpreting one particular clause is not direct authority for the interpretation of a similar, but not identical clause (*Equity and Law Life Assurance Society plc v Bodfield Ltd* [1987] 1 EGLR 124). The purpose of rent review is, however, very simple: to enable the landlord to grant a term of over, say, three years, while at the same time avoiding being tied to a rent which no longer reflects the level achievable in the open market. As Hoffman J said in *MFI Properties Ltd v BICC Group Pensions Trust Limited* [1986] 1 All ER 974:

> A rent review clause is designed to deal with a particular commercial problem, namely that of the tenant who wants security of tenure for a lengthy term, and the landlord who, in terms of inflation or a rapidly changing property market, does not want to commit himself to a fixed rent for the whole of that term.

The last decade has witnessed a move towards shorter leases, break clauses and other elements of flexibility in commercial leases, but rent reviews still have an important part to play. Thus, a lease will provide that the rent should be reviewed (usually upwards only) at intervals commonly of three or five years.

This may be achieved in a number of ways. The rent may be adjusted:

- by fixed amounts at stated intervals;
- by linking it to an index of prices such as the Retail Price Index;
- by linking it to the tenant's turnover;
- by linking it to the rent payable under a headlease or sub-lease of the property; or
- as is usually the case, by reviewing it at intervals to the current open market rent.

This type of clause will be the one dealt with in this book.

5.2   Contents

A rent review clause will typically make provision for:

• the timing of the review and the date on which the new rent will be payable;

• the machinery for initiating the review and for agreeing the new rent;

• the method of calculating the new rent; and

• the resolution of disputes.

5.3   Machinery for reviewing the rent

5.3.1 Trigger notices

Review clauses frequently contain provisions for initiating the review by service of a 'trigger' notice by the landlord, for the reaching of agreement between the parties and, finally, for the appointment of an arbitrator or expert to determine the rent in the absence of agreement, with each stage being governed by time limits. If a notice procedure is provided for, there may be provisions as to further notices which have to be served after the landlord's trigger notice, such as a tenant's counter-notice and, also, any notices relating to the appointment of the arbitrator or expert.

Alternatively, the review process my be automatic, the review clause stating that the rent may be agreed at any time between the parties but, in the absence of agreement, it will be fixed not earlier than the relevant review date by an arbitrator or expert agreed by the parties or nominated by the President of the RICS on the application of the landlord or the tenant not earlier than six months before the review date, and not later than the end of the review period.

5.3.2 Time limits

Where time limits are stipulated, the general rule is that time is not of the essence (*United Scientific Holdings Ltd v Burnley BC* [1978] AC 904). Thus, a party who fails to observe a time limit will not be prejudiced by his tardiness either in losing the right to review or to object to the other side's figure and, when the reviewed rent is fixed, will be able to recover it retrospectively (but only with interest if the lease so provides). There are certain exceptions to this general rule:

- ˙ where it is stated in the lease that time is of the essence;
- where there are other indications in the lease that time limits are strict. Thus, the lease may state that the landlord's trigger notice is a condition precedent to the review taking place (*Chelsea Building Society v R and A Millett (Shops) Ltd* [1994] 4 EG 182); the lease may stipulate a time limit and state 'but not otherwise' (*Drebbond v Horsham DC* (1978) 37 P&CR 237); or may be structured so that, at each stage, a certain consequence is deemed to flow from a failure to observe a time limit (*Henry Smith's Charity Trustees v AWADA Trading and Promotion Services Ltd* (1983) 47 P&CR 607). However, subtle differences in the drafting of the lease can lead to a different conclusion and this is, in consequence, the most difficult exception to apply;
- where the tenant serves a notice on the landlord making time of the essence, in situations where he has no other remedy. There is no prescribed form of notice and a letter will suffice provided that its intention is sufficiently clear;
- where there is a break clause (of which time limits are strict as a general rule) allowing the tenant to terminate the lease by serving a notice to quit after receiving a rent review notice (*Al Saloom v James Shirley Travel Services* (1981) 42 P&CR 181).

Practitioners will sometimes be involved in drafting landlords' trigger notices and tenants' counter-notices. This is critically important where time is, in fact, of the essence. On the renewal of such old leases, the landlord should take the opportunity of updating the rent review clause (s 34(3) of the 1954 Act).

5.4   Calculation of the new rent

5.4.1 Valuation formulae

Practitioners involved in drafting business leases must be aware of the effect that their handiwork (whether in the lease generally or in the review clause itself) can have on the rent achieved on review. A rent review clause invariably contains a mixture of assumptions and disregards, and a valuer acting in a rent review must inhabit the hypothetical world thereby created. Thus, a practitioner should, in anything but a standard case, consult with the landlord's surveyor at the drafting stage, or at least forward a copy of the draft lease for comment. The practitioner should also record the instructions from, and advice to, the client, and explain carefully and clearly to the client the rent review formula.

A specialist work, such as Reynolds, K, Featherstonhaugh, G and Bernstein, R, *Handbook of Rent Review* or Lewison, K, *Drafting Business Leases*, 5th edn, 1996, should be consulted to expand upon the brief outline stated here. The following points should be noted.

The variety of phrases used as valuation formula such as 'open market rent', 'rack rent' and 'reasonable rent' are capable of different meanings, but usually require an objective assessment of the rent. Thus, the term 'reasonable rent' was held in one case to mean not what was reasonable between the parties, but rather the rent at which the premises might reasonably be expected to be let in the open market. Thus, where there was no express disregard of the tenant's improvements, these had to be taken into account in fixing the rent review, however unreasonable this was from the tenant's point of view (*Ponsford v HMS Aerosols Ltd* [1979] AC 63, HL).

Despite this, in general, phrases such as 'reasonable rent' and 'fair rent' should be avoided, as they may allow the tenant to introduce personal factors. By contrast, a rent which it is reasonable for the tenant to pay may involve a consideration of the circumstances of the landlord and tenant, and a recognition that it would not be reasonable for the tenant to pay rents on improvements to the property for which he had paid (*Thomas Bates and Sons v Wyndhams Lingerie* [1981] 1 WLR 505).

The tenant should not accept the rent being reviewed to the 'best rent'. In some circumstances, this could be higher than the open market rent, as it allows the valuer to have regard to the fact that certain categories of prospective tenant may be willing to pay more than the market rent.

5.4.2 Assumptions and disregards

The review clause will state a number of factors – known as the 'assumptions' and 'disregards' which should either be taken into account or omitted when calculating the new rent. It is up to the parties themselves to decide which assumptions and disregards should be included when the lease is first negotiated.

Assumptions include:
- that the hypothetical lease has been granted by a willing landlord to a willing tenant. This presupposes that there is a market for the premises. Where they are functionally obsolete (as in *FR Evans (Leeds) Ltd v English Electric Co Ltd* (1977) 36 P&CR 185), the tenant may wish to amend this aspect of the review clause;

- that the premises are vacant. Although a review clause will normally provide that vacant possession is to be assumed, where there are to be sub-lettings, both sides should consider whether or not such an assumption is in their best interests from a valuation point of view. The lack of such an assumption may lead to uncertainty;

- that the hypothetical letting is for the term of the lease still to run. Generally, rental values will depreciate as the lease nears its end, though account should be taken of the possibility of it continuing or being renewed under the 1954 Act (see *Secretary of State for the Environment v Pivot Properties Ltd* [1980] 256 EG 1176). Thus, the landlord may provide in the draft lease that it will be assumed that rent is being assessed for the full original term. The tenant should argue that the actual residue should form the basis of the valuation. A compromise somewhere in the middle will sometimes result (for example, the residue of the term or a specified period of years, whichever is longer);

- that the tenant has fulfilled his obligations. There should be an express assumption that the tenant has observed all his obligations (though this would probably be implied, as in *Harmsworth Pension Fund Trustees Ltd v Charringtons Industrial Holdings Ltd* (1985) 49 P&CR 297) to make it absolutely clear that the tenant cannot benefit from his own breaches of covenant;

- that the hypothetical lease is on the same terms and conditions as the actual lease, other than the current rent, but including the review provisions. The tenant must be careful to ensure that the review clause does not require the valuer to disregard the fact that there are rent reviews. Thus, the rent on a 10 year lease without rent reviews would be higher than the rent at the commencement of such a term with a review after, say, five years. The review clause may avoid any potential problems in this regard by providing that the rent be assessed, 'subject to the terms of this lease (other than the amount of the rent hereby reserved but including the provisions for review of that rent)'. There would be potential uncertainty (though probably resolved in the tenant's favour following *British Gas Corporation v Universities Superannuation Scheme* [1986] 1 WLR 398) if the rent were instead to be fixed 'subject to the terms of this lease (other than those relating to rent)';

- that the whole premises are available for the permitted use under the lease. The estate management advantages of a narrow user clause can be outweighed by its depreciatory effect on a rent review and the valuer should take no account of the fact that the landlord may allow different uses unless the user restriction is a qualified one with an express reasonableness proviso (see *Plinth Property Investments v Mott, Hay and Anderson* (1978) 38 P&CR 361 and *Forte and Co v General Accident Life Assurance Ltd* [1986] 2 EGLR 115). A landlord may provide a narrow restriction on user, but state that a different, more profitable user is to be assumed for the purpose of rent review. The drafter of such a clause should expressly provide that the premises are assumed to be fit for the hypothetical user and that such user is lawful. The tenant should resist hypothetical user provisions if possible;

• that the property to be valued is whole of the demised property. Sometimes, however, the parties will fix the rent to a hypothetical building, usually where the actual building has been adapted to suit the tenant's needs. Clear words will be needed before the court will be able to conclude that the parties intended the valuation to be of part only of the property comprised in the lease (for example, the site of a building, but on the building itself);

• that the tenant is able to recover any VAT payable on the rent.

The express disregards usually follow those contained in s 34 of the 1954 Act, but should be adapted and set out in full. The practice of incorporating this section by reference has been criticised (*Brett v Brett Essex Golf Club Ltd* [1986] 278 EG 1476) and can lead to uncertainty.

Matters to be disregarded will include the effect on the rent of:

• the tenant being in occupation;

• the tenant's goodwill;

• the tenant's voluntary improvements. This is one of the most important disregards. The tenant should ensure that this disregard covers pre-lease improvements where relevant (see the *Brett Essex* case cited above). An improvement may be carried out by the tenant even if the work has been physically performed by a third party, provided that the tenant identifies, supervises and pays for the work (*Durley House Ltd v Cadogan* [2000] 1 WLR 246).

5.4.3 Rent-free periods

A tenant often obtains a rent-free period at the beginning of a lease to enable him to adapt the premises to his particular requirements and/or as an inducement to enter into a lease. The fact that such concessions exist in the market can have the effect of depressing the rent on review (see *99 Bishopsgate Ltd v Prudential Assurance Co Ltd* [1985] 273 EG 984). Drafting problems can arise with regard to eliminating the effect of such inducements. The best technique for the landlord wishing to achieve a non-discounted rent on review is to include an assumption that the rent is that payable after the expiry of any rent-free concession or fitting-out period (but not, then, to go on to disregard such concessions, as in *City Offices plc v Bryanston Insurance* [1993] 11 EG 129).

The whole question of the effect of inducements has become much more complex recently. In the very difficult letting market of recent years, landlords have been offering very significant rent-free periods (sometimes of a year or more) and other inducements to tempt tenants into signing leases. The figure paid by tenants after the expiry of such inducements is usually referred to as the 'headline rent'. Ordinarily, such inducements would be taken into account when assessing the actual rent achieved on such lettings, so that the 'market rent' on such a letting would be less than the 'headline rent'. However, in an attempt to maintain rental values, landlords started to draft rent review clauses in such a way as to attempt to disregard the effect of any such inducements, so that the 'market rent' of such a letting in the context of a rent review would be equal to the 'headline rent'.

The position in relation to such rent review clauses was clarified to some extent by the four Court of Appeal cases of *Co-operative Wholesale Society Limited v National Westminster Bank plc, Scottish Amicable Life Assurance Society v Middleton Potts and Co, Broadgate Square plc v Lehman Brothers Limited* and *Prudential Nominees Limited v Greenham Trading Limited*, all of which were heard together and reported at [1995] 01 EG 111.

In each of those cases, the landlord argued that the wording of the rent review clause required the third-party valuer to disregard all inducements available in the open market and, therefore, to apply the 'headline rent' achieved in comparable lettings. The Court of Appeal made it clear that the purpose of rent review clauses was to protect the landlord against the erosion in the value of money over the term of the lease. Giving effect to the landlord's contention would effectively give the landlord a significant windfall, as the rent on rent review would be significantly higher than the effective rent which could be obtained in the open market at the review date. Accordingly, the court would lean against construing a rent review clause to have that effect and only the clearest and most unambiguous wording would be interpreted as having that effect. Only in one of the four cases was the landlord's interpretation upheld.

Following those cases, it would appear that it is quite legitimate in a rent review clause to seek to prevent the tenant from arguing that he should obtain the benefit of a further fitting-out period on each review (unlike the hypothetical tenant, the actual tenant has already fitted out and does not need another fitting-out period before he is able to trade). However, any clause which seeks to go further than that and to disregard other inducements available in the market at the review date will be scrutinised very carefully by the courts. Only the most unambiguous clauses will be given this effect.

Generally, a rent-free period of up to three months will be regarded as being granted for fitting-out purposes and any longer period will be treated as an inducement. However, valuation advice should be sought from a surveyor whenever there is any doubt about the correct treatment of rent-free periods and other inducements.

Office precedents for leases generally, and review clauses in particular, need frequent revision. For example, solicitors should consider whether the landlord's right to elect to impose VAT upon rents could have a depreciatory effect on such rents. For the tenant who can recover this VAT, the only problem may be one of cash flow whereas, for the exempt or partially exempt tenant, VAT will represent a significant additional burden. Particularly for such exempt tenants, this could have the effect of reducing rents on the basis that such tenants cannot afford the usual rent plus an additional 17.5%. A surveyor's advice should be sought in specific cases.

Practitioners acting for landlords should be cautious in the light of cases on headline rent in attempting to insert assumptions and disregards to eliminate those depreciatory factors (see, for example, the cases of *City Offices plc v Bryanston Insurance* [1993] 11 EG 129) and the combined appeals in *Co-operative Wholesale Society Limited v National Westminster Bank plc* [1995] 01 EG 111).

5.5   Dispute resolution

Provision should always be made for the rent to be fixed by a surveyor in default of agreement, the actual person to be as agreed between the parties or otherwise as appointed by the President of the RICS. The RICS publish guidance notes which set out the procedure to be followed for the making of such an application. Their Dispute Resolution Service can be contacted at Surveyor Court, Westwood Way, Coventry, CV4 8JE (telephone 020 222 7000 or helpline number 020 7334 3806). The email address is drs@rics.org.uk.

The lease will state whether the surveyor appointed is to act as an arbitrator or an expert. An arbitration will be controlled by the Arbitration Act 1996, which provides for an appeal against an arbitration award in a rent review to the High Court on a point of law. In contrast, an expert's decision is final. Unlike an expert, an arbitrator is obliged to hear evidence and submissions from each party and is bound to reach a decision solely on the evidence presented. Only an arbitrator can order discovery of documents, attendance of witnesses and costs.

Arbitration should be the first choice of the person drafting the lease where rental income will be high, where the building is unusual, or where points of law may be involved. A surveyor may prefer to act as an arbitrator, as only then is he immune from an action in negligence. Appointment of an expert should be considered where the reviews are likely to be straightforward, and quick and conclusive decisions are required.

6 Drafting the Lease

In this chapter, only a brief commentary on some of the most important parts of a business lease is provided, but no attempt is made, for reasons of space, to provide a comprehensive list. Such precedents can be found in Aldridge, T, *Practical Lease Precedents*, London: Sweet & Maxwell. There is a danger that 'precedents stored electronically ... [may] accumulate further provisions over the years, rather like barnacles on the hull of a man-of-war' (Tromans, S, *Commercial Leases*, 2nd edition, 1996, p 4). Thus, a provision which is entirely appropriate when added in the context of a particular transaction should not necessarily always be applied thereafter.

6.1 The preamble

At the beginning of the lease, there may be a list of contents, the date, particulars containing details of the parties to the deed and other information which will vary with each letting, a clause defining frequently used terms and an interpretation clause which should state, amongst other things, that headings and marginal notes are to be disregarded. Terms used in one part of the lease only (such as the rent review clause) are more usefully defined at the beginning of the relevant part.

6.2 The description

Particular care should be taken with regard to the property description, especially where the lease is of part of a building, so that the full extent of repairing obligations can be determined. The description must deal precisely with both the horizontal and vertical boundaries and expert advice may be needed with regard to the method of construction of the building. There should usually be a professionally drawn plan on such a scale as to enable the exact position of the boundaries to be ascertained. If the verbal description is to prevail over the plan, then the plan should be expressed to be 'for identification purposes only'. It will usually be more appropriate for the plan to prevail and a phrase such as 'more particularly delineated on the plan' will be used. Avoid using both expressions at the same time, as is sometimes achieved in practice!

Incorporating a list of fixtures and fittings into the description can be of great assistance for the purposes of rent reviews and to determine the full extent of repairing obligations and the items the tenant can remove at the end of the lease.

6.3 Tenant's rights and landlord's exceptions and reservations

The need for easements and similar rights should be considered by both parties' solicitors. The lease will read more easily if use is made of schedules at the end of the lease rather than setting out such rights in detail after the property description.

The tenant will need not only a right of physical access, including, perhaps, a right to use a lift, but also rights in connection with services. The tenant may require a right of parking, a right to use sanitary facilities, a right of access to neighbouring properties to carry out repairs to the demised premises, and rights of light and air. Although such rights will often be implied, the tenant, in the interests of certainty, should require that they be granted expressly. Conversely, the landlord may wish to exclude certain rights, such as those relating to light and air, by providing that the landlord has an absolute right to develop his neighbouring property.

Although not strictly correct, the words 'exceptions' and 'reservations' are commonly grouped together to describe all easements and other rights which the landlord is to exercise over the demised premises. Such rights are sometimes drafted as covenants by providing that the tenant shall permit the landlord to do something, thereby enabling the landlord to threaten forfeiture if the tenant is obstructive. The rights will be similar to those granted to the tenant, but will also embrace much more far ranging rights of access to enable the landlord to enter to inspect the condition and state of repair and to carry out works to the demised and neighbouring premises. The tenant's solicitors should seek amendments to the draft lease, where necessary, to require the landlord to give reasonable notice before exercising such rights of access and to restore the premises where any damage has been caused.

The landlord must consider carefully the extent of a right to carry out works. If drawn too widely, then this may operate to the landlord's disadvantage at expiry of the lease in preventing the landlord from using ground (f) (see 4.6). The landlord should consider, as an alternative, providing a break clause allowing the landlord to determine the lease early where the requirements of ground (f) are satisfied. This redevelopment break clause will serve the same purpose as a right of entry, but will not prevent the use of ground (f) (see the precedent in Aldridge (referred to above). Where development is a real possibility, the landlord should consider excluding the 1954 Act.

The landlord will usually reserve the right to construct and use new pipes, wires, etc, on the demised premises for the benefit of its neighbouring premises. The landlord should also reserve the right to affix letting or sale boards to the premises near to the end of the term. Where the lease is longer than 21 years, the grant of easements to be exercised in the future, such as the right to lay and use pipes, should be limited to a perpetuity period not exceeding 80 years (s 1(1) of the Perpetuities and Accumulations Act 1964).

6.4   Length of the term

The actual date of commencement of the term should be stated by using a phrase such as 'from and including the 25th day of March 2001'. For convenience, the term is often stated to commence on the last rent payment day falling before the date of the lease and the tenant should ensure that the rent is payable from the latter date rather than the earlier payment day.

In old tenancies (see 3.1.2), it was important for the landlord to seek to define the term as including any statutory continuation as, otherwise, the original tenant will not be liable for rent arrears accumulated by an assignee once the original contractual term has ended (*City of London Corporation v Fell* [1993] 4 All ER 968). However, in relation to new tenancies, this will be much less important and may even be void as an attempt to evade the provisions of the 1995 Act.

6.5   Rent

The initial rent, and whether it is payable in advance or in arrears will be specified. In the absence of any indication, rent will be payable in arrears and most landlords will require it to be paid in advance. Rent is commonly stated to be payable by equal quarterly payments in advance on the usual quarter days, that is 25 March, 24 June, 29 September and 25 December.

The rent should be stated to be exclusive of VAT.

If the landlord insures the property or provides services, the premiums and service charges should be reserved as further rents enabling the landlord to forfeit more easily, or to levy distress if payments are not made. The remedy of distress is not available for a breach of covenant other than non–payment of rent.

The provisions for reviewing the rent are usually contained in a schedule. This is one of the most important aspects of a lease and is considered separately in Chapter 5.

6.6   Tenant's covenants

6.6.1 To pay rent

Landlords are vulnerable to a tenant deducting the amount of a claim against his landlord from future rent payments. The right to withhold rent should therefore be expressly excluded. It is not sufficient for the lease to require the tenant to pay rent 'without any deductions', but rather the tenant's right of set off should be expressly excluded (*Connaught Restaurants Ltd v Indoor Leisure Ltd* [1994] 4 All ER 834). The tenant will usually be required to covenant to pay interest on outstanding rent.

6.6.2 To pay and indemnify the landlord against rates, taxes, charges and other outgoings imposed upon the premises or their owner or occupier

This would embrace not only matters such as general and water rates, but less obvious items such as road and maintenance charges. For the avoidance of any doubt, the tenant should make an amendment to such a provision to the effect that the covenant does not relate to any tax liability of the landlord in respect of the rent or arising out of any dealing in the landlord's reversionary interest.

6.6.3 Not to assign underlet or part with possession of the premises

See Chapter 8. In the absence of any restriction, the landlord will lose control over who may occupy the premises It is common to bar completely the alienation of part of the premises, but to provide that assigning or underletting the whole is permissible with the landlord's prior written consent. By virtue of the 1927 Act, this may not be unreasonably withheld or delayed, even if this is not expressly stated.

The 1995 Act has modified s 19 of the 1927 Act and it is now possible for landlords to exercise much greater control over assignment of the premises. Landlords' solicitors will need to take detailed instructions as to whether the landlord wishes to impose specific conditions and circumstances subject to which consent to assign will be given (see 3.7). The valuation impact of these provisions must also be considered carefully.

6.6.4 Not to carry out alterations

See Chapter 8. This will usually be made permissible with the landlord's prior written consent, which may not be unreasonably withheld. A landlord will see some form of restriction as essential to avoid the tenant having a free hand in this regard (subject to the doctrine of waste).

The landlord may permit a qualified covenant, but avoid the statutory restrictions upon withholding consent to some extent by barring the tenant from applying for planning permission or carrying out development as defined for planning purposes. The tenant should try to have such a covenant deleted.

6.6.5 Not to change the user

See Chapter 8. The landlord's desire to control the user for estate management reasons and to obtain further control over assignments and sub-lettings should be weighed against the depreciatory effect of such a clause on rental values. If the lease permits a variation in the use of the premises with the landlord's consent, the tenant should require that such consent cannot be unreasonably withheld (as this will not be implied). A landlord will not wish to dispense entirely with controls, even if this merely involves barring certain undesirable uses, such as the sale of pornography.

6.6.6 To keep the premises in repair

Most landlords will wish to achieve a clear lease whereby uncertain expenditure (such as that incurred in repairing the premises) will be borne by the tenant. Where the demised premises forms part of a building, shopping centre or industrial estate, or some other larger unit, then the landlord will usually covenant to repair the structure and exterior (leaving the tenant with primary responsibility for the interior) and will recover the cost by way of service charge. The tenant should ensure that this obligation extends to the whole building, centre or estate. Even where the premises do not form part of a larger unit, the landlord should reserve the right to carry out repairs where the tenant fails to do so and to recover the cost as a debt (see 2.4). The tenant should resist a clause which appears to make it liable for improvements and should seek the exclusion from its repairing obligation of damage which would be covered by the landlord's insurance policy.

In the case of an old building, the tenant may seek to limit its obligations by covenanting to keep the premises in the same condition as at the beginning of the lease. A schedule recording such condition should be prepared by a surveyor and attached to the lease. In the case of a new building, the tenant will wish to exclude liability for inherent defects, which term should be defined in the lease.

Whoever is to be responsible for repairs, the lease should provide that liability will cease where rebuilding is unavoidably prevented by outside circumstances, such as an inability to obtain planning permission. Most importantly of all, the landlord and the tenant between them must be responsible for repair of the whole of the premises with no parts remaining where neither party is responsible, or conversely where both the landlord and the tenant are responsible for certain parts of the premises. Uncertainty can arise where the demised premises are inadequately described (see 6.2).

6.6.7 To pay the landlord's expenses incurred first, in taking any action in respect of the tenant's breach of covenant and, secondly, in the granting of the lease

The first will include the service of notices, as the landlord should not be left out of pocket with regard to such matters. The insertion of the second is a matter for negotiation (see 1.7.1).

6.6.8 To give written notice of a dealing with the premises

This is essential, for estate management reasons.

6.6.9 To comply with the landlord's regulations made from time to time

Such a covenant is common, but potentially very disadvantageous to the tenant. The tenant should at least seek that a proviso is added that the regulations cannot override or contradict the provisions of the lease, nor unreasonably restrict the tenant in its use of the premises.

6.7   Landlord's covenants

6.7.1 To give the tenant quiet enjoyment

This covenant is not usually worded to cover dispossession of the tenant by the true owner or by a superior landlord and it will be difficult for the tenant to have it extended to cover such matters. The tenant should, therefore, try to insist upon the landlord providing proof of its title and advise the tenant of the risks if the landlord will not co-operate in this regard (see 1.6.1).

6.7.2 To provide services

This should be inserted where the tenant is required to pay for services by way of a service charge (see 6.8).

6.7.3 To insure the premises

Leases usually provide for the landlord to insure against specific risks and such further risks as the landlord from time to time regards as appropriate (for example, terrorism cover is often now added to the list of specific risks) and for the tenant to reimburse the landlord with regard to the premiums. The tenant should ensure that there is such an obligation (or other satisfactory arrangement), that the policy is adequate as to the amount and the risks covered and that any shortfall has to be made up by the landlord, that the landlord is obliged to use the funds to reinstate the premises, and that the lease provides that, in the event of significant damage or destruction, rent will cease to be payable until the premises are reinstated. The tenant should also require that the policy be in joint names, or its interest noted on the policy. The former will give the tenant joint control over the spending of the money and the latter should at least mean that the tenant is informed by the insurers if the policy lapses.

Alternatively, the tenant may be required to insure with an approved company against specified risks to the full reinstatement value of the premises and to make up any deficiency out of its own money. Landlords will often not accept a rent abatement clause in this situation and the tenant should insure against its obligation to pay rent during a period where the premises are unusable. Whoever insures the premises, the lease should state who retains the insurance moneys if rebuilding or reinstatement proves to be impossible. The landlord may wish to provide that the money is retained by the landlord, whereas the tenant may argue that the money be shared in accordance with a stated formula (for example, in proportion with the value of their interests).

Insurance is an area of great importance, and both the landlord and the tenant will expect their professional advisers to be assiduous in protecting their respective interests. It is good practice for all the landlord's and tenant's obligations and rights in this regard to be dealt with in a separate insurance clause. Deficiencies in the insurance arrangements are then more likely to be picked up at the drafting stage and the parties to the lease can more easily find the relevant insurance provisions rather than (as is often the case) having to look at the tenant's covenants, the landlord's covenants and the provisos.

6.7.4 Not to let or permit or suffer neighbouring properties to be used for a competing business

In the absence of such a provision, a tenant of shop premises could be subjected to detrimental competition without having a remedy against the landlord (see *Port v Griffith* [1938] 1 All ER 295).

6.8   The service charge

Reference has already been made in this chapter to the concept of a clear lease. Where the premises form part of a building, shopping centre or industrial estate (described in this context as 'the larger unit') and common services will be provided, the landlord will (by using a schedule) list every service it may wish to provide. The landlord may then create a safety net, to catch any it has missed, by adding that the tenant must pay for any other service not otherwise mentioned, but supplied by the landlord. The tenant should consider the list carefully and try to eliminate items which it may feel are inappropriate, such as the cost of improvements or rectifying inherent defects. From a landlord's point of view, the 'safety net' provision is probably reasonable, but the tenant should safeguard itself with qualifications, such as that the service must benefit the tenant and that it should be a service for which the tenant would reasonably expect to have to pay.

The parties may feel that it is desirable to provide that the tenants contribute to a sinking fund to be available when required to pay for major expenditure, such as lift replacement. This should avoid the tenants having to suffer major fluctuations in payments which may otherwise mean that an assignee immediately has to pay a large sum for an item in respect of which the assignor has had the benefit, but not the cost of replacing. The tenant should ensure that the lease provides that the fund be held by the landlord upon trust for a perpetuity period of, say, 80 years, thereby preventing the money falling into the hands of creditors on the landlord's insolvency. However, sinking funds can have adverse tax consequences for both the landlord and the tenants, and specialist tax advice is needed before such a fund is created.

There are various ways in which each tenant's share of the burden may be calculated. From the landlord's point of view, a fixed percentage (but with provision for the percentage to be revised to accommodate any extension to the premises or to the larger unit) or a formula (perhaps using the floor area or rateable value of the premises in relation to the combined floor areas or rateable values of the larger unit) has the great advantage of certainty and ease of administration. However, some tenants may place a heavier burden upon services than others and the tenant may prefer a more flexible approach, such as that the tenant shall pay a reasonable or fair share with such proportion to be determined by an independent third party. To avoid any doubt, a tenant will wish to include an express provision that the tenant is not to bear any portion of the service charge attributable to unlet premises.

The landlord will invariably wish to provide that payments be made in advance based on an estimate with any shortfall or overpayment to be paid or repaid once the actual cost for that year has been determined. The lease will usually provide that this final figure should be certified by a surveyor or accountant acting for the landlord. A court has the power to review the decision of an expert, certainly on matters of law (*Mercury Communications Ltd v Director General of Telecommunications* [1996] 1 WLR 48, HL). A landlord will still wish to state in the lease that the certificate is final as to questions of fact. It is also important that, if the landlord's surveyor or accountant is given a role in determining the appropriate amount, such person must be separate from the landlord or, alternatively, the lease should make it clear that the landlord's employees can fit this description. Otherwise, the certificate may be held to be void (*Finchbourne v Rodrigues* [1976] 3 All ER 581).

It is in both parties' interests that the landlord covenants to provide certain services and states whether others are provided at the landlord's discretion. The absence of such a provision will lead to uncertainty as to whether such an obligation will be implied (see *Duke of Westminster v Guild* [1985] QB 688).

6.9   Provisos

6.9.1 Re-entry

The landlord will insert a forfeiture clause into a fixed term lease providing that, if the tenant does not pay rent (whether formally demanded or not), or breaches some other covenant or condition or becomes bankrupt or enters into liquidation, then the landlord can take possession of the premises. No such rights of forfeiture will be implied.

The proviso for re-entry on the tenant's bankruptcy or liquidation will inhibit the use of the lease as security for a loan and the tenant should try to have this part of the forfeiture clause deleted. The tenant's chances of achieving this are low, save where the lease is at a premium and at a low rent, or is otherwise for a long term.

6.9.2 Suspension of rent

The tenant should insist that the lease contains a proviso that the rent be suspended in circumstances where the premises are unfit for use. The landlord may wish to restrict this to situations where the unfitness arises from destruction and damage by insured risks, save where the cover has been vitiated by the tenant's act, neglect or default. The tenant should insist that the landlord insures against all insurable risks. The tenant should try to ensure that the abatement applies also to matters arising outside of the premises, rendering them unusable, such as destruction of the main access. It will be a matter for negotiation whether other items commonly reserved as rent (such as insurance premiums and service charge payments) are also to be suspended. The tenant should resist any limitation of the rent abatement to a fixed period of perhaps three years, especially where the landlord has not covenanted to reinstate the premises. Otherwise, after this period has elapsed, the landlord may lose any incentive to restore the property.

6.9.3 Frustration

The lease may contain a proviso permitting the tenant (and possibly the landlord) to bring the lease to an end by notice where the premises have been unfit for a certain period of time. Otherwise, the tenant (and landlord) will have to rely upon the doctrine of frustration applying to terminate the lease in such circumstances which would be a matter of some uncertainty (see *National Carriers Ltd v Panalpina (Northern) Ltd* [1981] AC 675). The tenant should insist on such a proviso being inserted into the lease where the landlord has limited the rent abatement to a fixed period.

6.9.4 Options

The following points should be noted with regard to options contained in leases:

- where a tenant's option is stated to be conditional upon payment of rent and/or observance of other covenants, even a minor breach will deprive the tenant of the opportunity of exercising such option (*Bairstow Eves (Securities) Ltd v Ripley* (1992) 65 P&CR 220). The tenant's solicitor should resist the insertion of such a condition or seek to qualify it when negotiating the terms of the lease;

- it seems that service of an option notice will create a binding contract and, therefore, that drafting devices, such as providing for a signed counter-notice in the lease, are unnecessary (*Spiro v Glencrown Properties* [1991] 2 WLR 931);

- a notice exercising an option to determine served by the landlord must comply with s 25 of the 1954 Act or two notices must be served: one to exercise the break clause and the other to comply with the statutory requirements;

- an option to determine relating to only part of the property subject to a 1954 Act tenancy is ineffective (*Southport Old Links Ltd v Naylor* [1985] 273 EG 767);

- an option to renew and an option to purchase the reversion are registrable as Class C(iv) land charges and will be void against a purchaser of the reversion on a failure to register. Where the land is registered, the option should be protected by notice or caution (see also 2.6.)

6.9.5 Exclusion of compensation

The tenant's right to compensation under the 1954 Act, where the landlord has proved certain grounds for possession, can be excluded in essence where the period of business occupation will have been less than five years by the date on which the tenant is to leave the premises (s 38(2) and (3)). The landlord will not only wish to insert a proviso excluding these rights where the lease is for less than five years, but also where it is for a longer period, on the basis that it may still be effective if the landlord operates a break clause or there has been a change in the tenant and type of business during the term.

6.9.6 Contracting out

An agreement excluding the 1954 Act with the court's consent must be contained in or endorsed on the lease (s 38(4)). This is most conveniently done by a suitably worded proviso, for example:

> Having been authorised in this regard by an order of the Marton on Tyne County Court (No 1234) dated the First day of January 2001 made pursuant to a joint application by the Landlord and the Tenant under the Landlord and Tenant Act 1954 s 38(4) the Landlord and the Tenant agree that the provisions of the Landlord and Tenant Act 1954 ss 24–28 inclusive shall be excluded in relation to the tenancy created by this Lease.

7 Procedural Checklists

The following checklists are provided to give practitioners an illustration of the procedural steps to be taken on the grant, assignment and surrender of a business lease. They are not intended to be definitive or comprehensive. It is accepted that other practitioners may take different steps or take the same steps in a different order. Some court procedures are touched upon elsewhere in this book (see Chapter 9).

7.1 Grant of lease

7.1.1 Taking instructions and other preliminary matters

Acting for the landlord

(1) Basic details are obtained from the landlord and the agent negotiating the grant, including the identity of the tenant and his solicitor, the address of the property, the term, rent, premium, etc, the whereabouts of the title deeds, and whether the tenant is to pay the landlord's legal (and other) costs. It must be ascertained whether the landlord is satisfied as to the tenant's financial status, or whether references should be requested (these will more commonly be obtained by the estate agent). The landlord should be asked for a plan of the premises sufficient for search purposes and for all correspondence relating to the proposed terms of the lease. Suggest that all future written communications should be via yourself to avoid the danger of an enforceable contract coming into existence.

(2) Write to the tenant's solicitor confirming your instructions, enclosing a plan for the purposes of the tenant's searches, stating that all correspondence up to exchange of contracts (if any) or completion by exchange of lease and counterpart is subject to contract and lease, and asking for confirmation that the tenant will pay the landlord's costs (if this is to be the case).

(3) Obtain the deeds and examine them, amongst other things, to check ownership, the property description, easements, covenants, mortgages and other third party rights and any superior leases for restrictions on sub-letting and consider whether it is necessary or appropriate to deduce title or to have a contract. If the landlord's title is registered, obtain office copy entries.

(4) If there is a mortgage, check whether the landlord's power of leasing is restricted and, if so, write to the mortgagee for consent to the proposed lease.

(5) Take the landlord's detailed instructions on the terms of the lease, advising the landlord of the various alternative covenants and other matters which should be covered, perhaps using a standard form of lease as a guide. Advise the landlord that (subject to the provisions of the 1995 Act) he can remain liable on its covenants throughout the term (even after the disposal of the reversionary interest) and whether it is necessary or appropriate to deduce title (see 1.6.1) or have a contract (see 1.4.2). Explain to the landlord the effect of the 1954 Act and obtain instructions as to whether there is to be a contracting out of the security of tenure provisions. Advise the landlord with regard to the tax position including the right to elect to charge VAT on rents and premiums (see 1.8). Discuss with the landlord whether a schedule of the present condition of the property should be obtained and attached to the lease (see 6.6.6). Obtain a list of fixtures and fittings from the landlord. Arrange with the landlord for professionally drawn plans to be prepared.

(6) Make a site inspection if this is convenient and likely to be helpful.

(7) Make a full company search against a corporate tenant whose substance is unknown, to ascertain their financial position in relation to their obligations under the proposed lease, and discuss with the landlord whether there should be a guarantor or rent deposit.

(8) If the grant is of a sub-lease, check the headlease to see, amongst other things, if it contains terms affecting the proposed underletting, such as a user restriction or a requirement that the landlord's consent first be obtained, or even that there is an absolute bar on sub-letting. Ensure that the proposed underletting is for a shorter term than that created by the headlease and advise the landlord that he may lose his right to a new lease of the sub-let parts under the 1954 Act (see 4.7). If the head landlord's consent is required, ascertain his requirements for giving consent (including payment of costs) and provide details of referees (if required).

Acting for the tenant

(1) Obtain basic details from the tenant and the agent negotiating the grant, including the identity of the landlord and his solicitor, the address of the property, the term, rent, premium, etc, and whether the tenant is to pay the landlord's legal (and other) costs. Ask the tenant to let you have all correspondence relating to the proposed terms of the lease and suggest that all future written communications should be via yourself to avoid the danger of an enforceable contract coming into existence.

(2) Write to the landlord's solicitor stating that all correspondence up to exchange of contracts (if any) or completion by exchange of lease and counterpart is subject to contract and lease, and (if authorised by the tenant) confirm that the tenant will be responsible for the landlord's costs. Where an undertaking for costs is being given to the landlord's solicitor, consider obtaining an equivalent amount from the tenant to cover the undertaking.

(3) Take the tenant's detailed instructions on the terms of the lease, checking any information received from the landlord's solicitor or surveyor negotiating the grant. Advise the tenant that the landlord's own title should be deduced (see 1.6.1) and whether there should be a contract (see 1.4.2). Explain to the tenant the effect of the 1954 Act and obtain instructions as to whether there is to be a contracting out. Advise the tenant with regard to the tax position, including the landlord's right to elect to charge VAT on rents and premiums (see 1.8). Discuss with the tenant whether a schedule of the present condition of the property should be obtained and attached to the lease (see 6.6.6) and, in any event, advise the tenant of the need for a survey. Ascertain whether a mortgage offer is needed before the tenant exchanges contracts (if relevant) or completes the lease.

(4) Make a site inspection if this is convenient and likely to be helpful.

(5) Make a full company search against a corporate landlord whose substance is unknown and which has significant obligations under the lease to repair or provide other services, and discuss with the tenant whether there should be a guarantor of the landlord's obligations.

(6) If the grant is of a sub-lease, obtain a copy of the headlease from the landlord's solicitor and check the matters in para (8) of the landlord's checklist above (where appropriate). Ascertain if the head landlord will require references before granting a licence to sub-let and request details of referees from the tenant (if required).

7.1.2 Up to completion

Acting for the landlord

(1)   Draft the lease and obtain the landlord's approval before submitting it to the tenant's solicitor in duplicate. If there is to be a contract, draft and submit this to the tenant's solicitor in duplicate at the same time. The draft lease will be attached to the contract. If title is to be deduced, submit an abstract or epitome back to a good root of title, or (if the title is registered) office copy entries.

(2)   In consultation with the landlord, reply to the list of preliminary inquiries submitted by the tenant's solicitor.

(3)   Consider the amendments to the draft lease (and contract) made by the tenant's solicitor and, in consultation with the landlord, re-amend this draft document in green (or other different colour).

(4)   If a sub-lease is involved, forward the tenant's references to the head landlord and submit to the tenant's solicitor the draft licence to sublet prepared by the head landlord's solicitor. Amend or approve the form of licence, have the licence executed by the landlord and the tenant (if required), and exchange parts with the head landlord's solicitor before exchange of contracts or (if there is no contract or if the contract was entered into conditionally upon the licence being obtained) before completion.

(5)   If relevant, send the approved draft lease to the landlord's mortgagee for approval and obtain a letter of consent to the letting before exchange of contracts or (if none) before completion.

(6)   Write to the landlord, summarising and advising the landlord with regard to the terms of the lease and confirming advice given orally on various matters. A copy of the final form of lease should be sent to the landlord.

(7)   If the tenancy is not to be protected by the security of tenure provisions of the 1954 Act, prepare and make the appropriate joint application and obtain a court order under s 38(4) before there is a binding contract, or exchange contracts conditionally upon the obtaining of the order (see 4.4 and the Precedents in 9.2).

(8)   If relevant, have the contract signed by the landlord and attached draft lease initialled, and exchange contracts, receiving an agreed proportion (usually 10%) of any premium payable.

(9)   Have the draft lease engrossed in two parts, send the counterpart to the tenant's solicitor to be executed by the tenant and have

the lease executed by the landlord in escrow in readiness for completion.

(10)   Calculate the first rent payment (usually up to the next quarter day). Send a completion statement to the tenant's solicitor incorporating the first rent payment and (if relevant) the property insurance premium, interim service charge payment, the balance of any premium payable (after taking any deposit paid into account) and the landlord's fees.

(11)   Complete by handing over the lease and mortgagee's letter of consent (if applicable) in exchange for the counterpart lease and sum due as per the completion statement. If requested, the landlord's solicitor may mark copies or an abstract of his unregistered title deeds as examined against the originals as agent for the tenant.

Acting for the tenant

(1)   Acknowledge receipt of the draft lease, check that its terms broadly accord with the tenant's instructions and send a copy to the tenant.

(2)   Send a form of inquiries to the landlord's solicitor appropriate to the grant of a lease to ascertain information such as the planning history of the premises and details of the property insurance policy. Request details of the landlord's title and copies of all documents referred to in the draft lease. Raise requisitions once title has been deduced, including a request that the landlord's mortgagee's consent be obtained before exchange of contracts or (if none) before completion. If the landlord's title is registered and the proposed lease is for a term in excess of 21 years, ask the landlord to deposit his land certificate at the Land Registry on completion and to advise you of the deposit number in order that the lease can be registered.

(3)   Request a local search and inquiries of the appropriate local authority. If the landlord's title has not been deduced or is unregistered, make an index map search at HM Land Registry. Make other searches as appropriate, such as common land and coal-mining searches.

(4)   Read the draft lease carefully, making appropriate amendments in red. Discuss and explain the lease in detail with the tenant before making final amendments. If these will be of a fundamental nature, obtaining the landlord's solicitor's agreement to the desired changes before making detailed amendments may save much wasted effort.

(5)   Return one copy of the amended lease to the landlord's solicitor and suggest that it be used as a 'travelling draft'. This may pass to and fro several times before agreement is reached.

(6)   If a sub-lease is involved, send the tenant's references to the landlord's solicitor, consider and amend the draft licence to underlet, have the engrossed licence executed by the tenant (if required) and return it to the landlord's solicitor duly executed. Ensure that the licence has been granted before exchange of contracts (if relevant), or make exchange conditional.

(7)   Consider the replies to inquiries and searches and the draft lease and forward a written report to the tenant. This should summarise and advise the tenant with regard to the terms of the lease and any matters arising from the searches and inquiries and confirm advice given orally on various matters. A copy of the final form of lease should be sent to the tenant.

(8)   Check the details of the property insurance and ensure that this will be in force by the time contracts are exchanged or the lease completed (if no contract is envisaged).

(9)   If relevant, have the contract signed by the tenant and attached draft lease initialled. Send the tenant's part of the contract to the landlord's solicitor with the agreed deposit once you and the tenant are satisfied that everything is in order, including the financial arrangements.

(10)   Final searches should be made. A search at the Companies Registry against a corporate landlord will ascertain whether there are any floating or fixed charges (pre–1970 fixed charges are binding, even if not registered under the Land Charges Act 1972) and, in the case of registered or unregistered land, will ensure that no resolution to put the company into voluntary liquidation has been passed and that it has not been removed from the register. Full land charges searches should be made against the name of the landlord and previous estate owners or, if appropriate, a registered land search made from the date of office copy entries supplied.

(11)   When the engrossed counterpart lease is received, check this against the amended draft lease and have it executed by the tenant in escrow.

(12)   Check the completion statement received from the landlord's solicitor and obtain the balance required to complete from the tenant.

(13)   Complete the lease as in the landlord's checklist para (11) (7.1.2).

7.1.3 Post-completion steps

Acting for the landlord

(1)   Pay £5 stamp duty upon the counterpart lease.

(2)   Pay the estate agent's bill, if authorised by the landlord.

(3)   Account to the landlord for the premium, first rent payment and any other money received.

(4)   If a sub-letting is involved, give notice of the underlease to the head landlord and retain a receipted copy notice with the underlease.

(5)   Arrange for the tenant's interest to be noted on the landlord's insurance policy if requested by the tenant.

(6)   If appropriate and not attended to before completion, lodge the land certificate at the Land Registry to enable the tenant to note his interest.

(7)   Lodge the counterpart lease with the deeds or otherwise in accordance with the landlord's wishes.

Acting for the tenant

(1)   If the title is unregistered, protect an option to renew or purchase the reversion by registration of a C(iv) land charge against the landlord's name.

(2)   Pay ad valorem stamp duty on the lease within 30 days of completion. Where there is an agreement for a lease, duty is paid on the agreement, but this will generally be submitted at the same time as the lease (see 1.9). Where the lease is for seven years or more, particulars must be delivered within the same period (see 1.9).

(3)   Give notice to the landlord of any mortgage of the lease entered into by the tenant and retain a receipted copy notice with the lease.

(4)   If the lease is for more than 21 years, apply for first registration within two months of completion. To preserve priority, this should be done within the priority period shown in the registered land search, and also the lease must be noted on the Charges Register of the landlord's title. The Registrar should be reminded to protect an option to renew or purchase the reversion by entry of a separate notice on the landlord's title (though this will usually be done automatically).

(5)   Send the lease and other deeds to the tenant's mortgagee and send copies to the tenant. If there is no mortgage, send the deeds to the client, or elsewhere in accordance with his instructions.

7.2   Assignment of lease

7.2.1 Taking instructions and other preliminary matters

Acting for the assignor

(1)   Obtain basic details from the assignor and the agent negotiating the assignment, including the identity of the assignee and his solicitor, the whereabouts of the title deeds and whether the tenant is to pay all the landlord's legal costs and/or those incurred in obtaining the licence to assign. If the assignor is also assigning the goodwill of the business carried on from the premises and the fixtures and fittings, ask him to discuss with his accountant the appropriate apportionment between the leasehold estate, the goodwill and the fixtures and fittings and to provide a list of the latter. Ask the assignor to let you have a plan of the premises, the receipt for the last rent payment and details and receipts for service or maintenance charge payments for, say, the last three years, and all correspondence relating to the proposed assignment. Suggest that all future written communications should be via yourself to avoid the danger of an enforceable contract coming into existence.

(2)   Write to the assignee's solicitor confirming your instructions, enclosing a plan for the purposes of the assignee's searches, stating that all correspondence up to formal exchange of contracts is subject to contract, or that you do not have authority to enter into a contract on your client's behalf, and seeking confirmation that the assignee is responsible for your costs and/or those of the landlord (if this is the case).

(3)   Obtain the title deeds and examine them to check the lease and superior titles, amongst other things, for restrictions on assignment and change of use, the property description and the existence of mortgages and consider to what extent it is necessary or appropriate to deduce superior titles (see 1.6.2). If the assignor's title is registered, obtain office copy entries of the register.

(4)   Ascertain the landlord's requirements with regard to giving consent to the assignment (if relevant).

(5)   Take the assignor's detailed instructions with regard to the terms of the contract, including apportionments where the goodwill is also to be assigned. Ascertain whether there are any rent arrears or other breach of covenant, especially relating to repairs. Advise the assignor that, although the contract and assignment will exclude liability for disrepair, this may still be a matter for

negotiation, especially if the landlord refuses to give consent to the assignment unless satisfactory arrangements to deal with breaches of covenant are made. Explain that, where the assignor has paid a service charge in advance on the basis of estimated figures, the apportionment made on completion can only be provisional. The contract should provide that the assignor or assignee will pay any balance or excess due when the actual amount is ascertained. The assignor or assignee may want the contract to make provision for a sum to be put aside to cover this or for some other arrangements to be made.

Advise the assignor of the importance of investigating the financial standing of the assignee, as the assignor may still be liable for future breaches of covenant. This is particularly important where the lease being assigned is an old tenancy (see 3.1.2), where the assignor will generally remain liable for the remainder of the term. In relation to new tenancies, if the landlord requires an AGA from the assignor (see 3.1.3), he will remain liable only until the assignee (lawfully) assigns the lease. In some cases, a rental deposit or guarantee (whether or not also required by the landlord) may be appropriate. Explain the tax implications of the assignment. Ascertain the approximate amount owing on any mortgages and ensure that there is sufficient to redeem them.

(6)   Make a full company search against a corporate assignee whose substance is unknown to ascertain their financial position, and ask the assignee's solicitors for referees or references whether or not required by the landlord in connection with giving consent to the assignment.

Acting for the assignee

(1)   Obtain basic details from the assignee and the agent negotiating the assignment, including the identity of the assignor and his solicitor, and whether the assignee is to pay all the assignor's legal costs and/or those incurred in obtaining the licence to assign. Ask the assignee for all correspondence relating to the proposed assignment and suggest that all future written communications should be via yourself to avoid the danger of an enforceable contract coming into existence.

(2)   Write to the assignor's solicitor stating that all correspondence up to formal exchange of contracts is subject to contract, or that you do not have authority to enter into a contract on your client's behalf, and (if authorised by the assignee) confirming the costs for which the assignee will be responsible. Where an undertaking

for costs is being given to the assignor's solicitor, consider obtaining an equivalent amount from the assignee to cover the undertaking.

(3)   Take the assignee's detailed instructions and advise the assignee on similar (but not identical) matters to those in para (5) of the assignor's checklist (7.2.1) and para (3) of the tenant's checklist (7.1.1).

(4)   Make a site inspection if this is convenient and likely to be helpful.

(5)   Provide details of referees or references to the assignor's solicitor.

(6)   Make a full company search against a corporate landlord whose substance is unknown, to ascertain their financial position in relation to their obligations under the lease.

7.2.2 Up to completion

Acting for the assignor

(1)   Draft the contract and submit it to the assignee's solicitor in duplicate, together with a copy of the lease and assignments back to a good root, or (if title is registered) a copy of the lease and office copy entries of the register together with (whether or not the leasehold title is registered) evidence of superior titles (if these are to be deduced).

(2)   In consultation with the assignor, reply to the list of preliminary inquiries submitted by the assignee's solicitor.

(3)   Forward the assignee's references or other information required to the landlord and submit to the assignee's solicitor the draft licence to assign prepared by the landlord's solicitor. Amend or approve the form of licence, have the licence executed by the assignor and the assignee (if required) and exchange parts with the landlord's solicitor before exchange of contracts or completion if the contract was entered into conditionally upon the licence being completed.

(4)   Agree the form of contract with the assignee's solicitor, have one part of the approved contract signed on behalf of the assignor, and exchange contracts, receiving an agreed proportion (usually 10%) of the consideration.

(5)   If the full title to which the assignee is entitled was not disclosed before exchange of contracts, forward an epitome/abstract or office copy entries to the assignee's solicitor.

(6)   Reply to any requisitions on title raised by the assignee's solicitor and return one copy of the draft assignments of the leasehold estate and goodwill (if applicable) approved or amended.

(7)   Obtain a redemption figure from any mortgagee holding a charge over the leasehold estate and obtain a letter of non-crystallisation from the chargee with regard to any floating charge.

(8)   Calculate apportionments of rent and service charge payments from the completion date until the next payment dates and possibly general and water rates and an interim payment for stock (if relevant) pending a final valuation on the day of completion and send a completion statement to the assignee's solicitor requiring payment of the above, any fees agreed to be paid, such as the landlord's solicitor's, and the balance of the price after taking into account any deposit paid.

(9)   Have the engrossed assignment executed by the assignor in escrow.

(10)   The assignment is completed by handing over the lease, assignment, land certificate or other unregistered title deeds, licence to assign, letter of non-crystallisation (if there is a floating charge) and an undertaking to redeem any charges in exchange for the sum due as per the completion statement. If relevant, give the appropriate sum to the mortgagee to redeem a charge.

Acting for the assignee

(1)   Consider the draft contract, lease and other title details supplied and send a list of preliminary inquiries to the assignor's solicitor, including a request for a full disclosure of superior titles.

(2)   Request a local search and inquiries of the appropriate local authority. Make an index map search at HM Land Registry and a land charges search against the names of estate owners disclosed, whether in connection with the assignor's title or superior titles (if such titles are unregistered). Make other searches as appropriate, including common land and coal-mining searches.

(3)   Discuss and explain to the assignee the contract, lease and draft licence to assign and all information obtained from your investigations, inquiries and searches. Where the lease is an old tenancy (see 3.1.2), the licence will almost certainly be drafted so as to make the assignee liable throughout the term (see 8.2.4). Where the lease is a new tenancy, explain to the assignee the provisions of the AGA (where one is required by the landlord) (see 3.1.3).

(4)   Return one part of the contract and the draft licence to the assignor's solicitor either approved as drawn or subject to amendments made to the drafts. If the lease contains fundamental defects, then it may be appropriate to insist that the assignor negotiates amendments with the landlord before proceeding.

(5)   Forward a written report to the assignee summarising and advising the assignee with regard to the matters discussed and explained as mentioned in (3) above, and confirming advice given orally. A copy of the lease should be sent to the assignee.

(6)   Check the insurance arrangements to ensure that the assignee will be protected from exchange of contracts.

(7)   Have the licence to assign executed by the assignee (if required) and the contract signed.

(8)   If you and the assignee are satisfied that everything is in order, including the financial arrangements, and the licence has been granted, exchange contracts by forwarding the assignee's part of the contract plus a solicitor's client account cheque for the agreed deposit to the assignor's solicitor. If the licence has not yet been completed, exchange must be conditional upon this being obtained.

(9)   Consider any further title details supplied, raise requisitions on title, and draft the assignments of the leasehold estate and goodwill (if applicable), submitting these to the assignor's solicitor.

(10)   Company searches should be made against a corporate landlord and assignor. Full land charges searches should be made against the assignor landlord and previous estate owners not already the subject of searches (if relevant). Make a land registry search from the date of office copy entries supplied where the title is registered.

(11)   Have the approved draft assignment(s) engrossed and executed by the assignee and forward these to the assignor's solicitor in escrow for execution by the assignor.

(12)   Check the computations contained in the assignor's completion statement and send a statement to the assignee showing the balance required to complete, and your own fees and disbursements, including those to be incurred, such as registration fees and stamp duty. To complete the assignment, hand over the sum due in exchange for the documents referred to in para (10) of the assignor's checklist.

7.2.3 Post-completion steps

Acting for the assignor

(1)   Pay the estate agent's bill if authorised by the assignor.

(2)   Account to the assignor for the net sale proceeds.

(3)   If relevant, have the mortgage deed receipted or Form 53 sealed

by the mortgagee and give notice to the landlord. Forward the deed or Form 53 and receipted copy notice to the assignee's solicitor.

Acting for the assignee

(1) Pay ad valorem stamp duty on the assignment and, where the term is for seven years or more, deliver particulars to the Inland Revenue, both within 30 days of completion.

(2) Give notice to the landlord of the assignment of the lease (and mortgage if appropriate) and retain receipted copy notice(s) with the deeds.

(3) If the assignment is of a lease having more than 21 years to run, apply for first registration within two months of completion. If the leasehold title is registered, apply for registration of the dealing within the priority period shown in the registered land search to preserve priority.

(4) Send the deeds to the assignee's mortgagee. If there is no mortgagee, send the deeds to the assignee or elsewhere, in accordance with his instructions.

7.3 Surrender

The procedural steps are here considered from both parties' points of view.

(1) The terms of the surrender are confirmed in correspondence marked 'subject to contract'.

(2) The landlord's solicitor will ask the tenant's solicitor to provide an epitome or abstract of his leasehold title and to confirm that there is no mortgage or charge affecting that title, or to supply office copy entries. The tenant's solicitor should investigate the landlord's title in the same way. Where the landlord's or tenant's legal estates are mortgaged, the mortgagee should be asked to join in as a party to the deed of surrender to give his consent. Alternatively, a mortgage of the lease may be discharged before completion or, in the case of a mortgage of the landlord's reversion, a letter of consent to the surrender may suffice.

(3) If an agreement to surrender is required, then the approval of the court must be obtained on the joint application of the landlord and tenant under s 38(4) of the 1954 Act, unless the lease is unprotected by that legislation. Otherwise, the agreement is void

under s 38(1).

(4)   The landlord's solicitor will submit a draft deed of surrender to the tenant's solicitor in duplicate for approval. It is important where the landlord is to receive any consideration that the deed states that VAT is payable on the consideration (see 1.8.1). Once approved, the landlord's solicitor will engross it in duplicate, having the counterpart sealed by the landlord and sending the deed of surrender to the tenant's solicitor for execution by the tenant.

(5)   The landlord's solicitor will send a completion statement to the tenant's solicitor detailing the sums due on completion. This will usually involve a premium to be paid to the landlord or tenant and will also show any rent and service charge payments apportioned up to the date of surrender. The agreement (or the deed of surrender itself, where there is no agreement) should provide that the landlord or tenant will pay any balance or excess due when the actual amount is ascertained.

(6)   Both the landlord's and the tenant's solicitors should make land charges searches and (if relevant) company searches or search the register of title from the date of the office copy entries supplied.

(7)   On completion, the landlord will receive the lease and other deeds held by the tenant, together with the deed of surrender executed by the tenant. The tenant will receive the counterpart lease and deed of surrender. The sum stated in the completion statement will be handed over to the landlord or tenant as appropriate.

(8)   If the lease is registered, the deed of surrender should take the form of a transfer to the registered proprietor or owner of the superior estate. An application should be made to register the surrender by forwarding to the Land Registry the land certificate (or charge certificate and evidence of discharge of the charge) relating to the registered lease and the lease and counterpart. Any notice of deposit or caution must be removed. If the superior title is registered, the land certificate relating to that title must be lodged to enable the notice of the lease to be cancelled. If that title is unregistered, then an examined abstract or epitome should be produced to the Registry. The register will be closed and certificate cancelled with regard to the leasehold title.

(9)   If the lease is unregistered but noted on the registered superior title, application for cancellation of the notice will be made on Form 92 accompanied by the land certificate of the superior estate and the deeds relating to the leasehold estate.

8 Landlord's Consent

8.1 General

At common law, the tenant has the right to assign or sub-let the demised premises, but the landlord will usually want to restrict the tenant's freedom of disposition. It must be appreciated, however, that extensive control over the right to alienate can significantly affect the amount which the landlord can expect to obtain by way of a premium or rent, either on granting the tenancy or on the occasion of a subsequent rent review.

8.1.1 Absolute or qualified

A covenant precluding assignment and sub-letting (alienation), alterations or a change of user may be expressed as an absolute restriction, or be qualified by requiring the landlord's prior consent. Various statutes, in particular the Landlord and Tenant Acts of 1927 and 1988 and the Landlord and Tenant (Covenants) Act 1995, affect the legal position where a tenant seeks the consent of the landlord to any of these matters.

A simple covenant against assignment will prohibit the tenant from legally assigning the residue of the tenancy in the whole of the premises by way of assignment. If the landlord also wishes to prohibit an assignment of part of the premises, the wording of the covenant should be extended accordingly. Otherwise, only an assignment of the whole will be prohibited. An involuntary assignment or an assignment by operation of law is not a breach of covenant against assignment.

A simple covenant against sub-letting will prohibit a sub-letting of the whole, but not part, of the premises (*Wilson v Rosenthal* (1906) 22 TLR 233). Thus, a sub-letting of part would not be a breach of such a covenant unless the sub-tenant had already sub-let the rest and the effect of the most recent sub-letting was that the whole was now sub-let (*Chatterton v Terrell* [1923] AC 578). Thus, the landlord who wants to prohibit a sub-letting of part should ensure that the covenant is so drafted. A covenant 'not to assign or underlet any part of the premises' will be breached by the assignment or sub-letting of the whole, because the disposal of the whole necessarily involves a disposition of part (*Field v Barkworth* [1986] 1 All ER 362).

	Absolute	**Qualified**
Alienation	The landlord can refuse consent on any ground whatsoever.★	The landlord's consent cannot be unreasonably withheld (s 19(1) of the 1927 Act), or delayed (s 1(2) of the 1988 Act). A fine cannot be required as a condition for giving consent other than reasonable expenses (s 144 of the LPA 1925). In relation to the assignment (but no other forms of alienation) of new tenancies (see 3.1.2) under the 1995 Act, the landlord may state in the lease specific circumstances in which his consent may be withheld and specific conditions subject to which his consent may be granted (see 3.7).
Alterations	The landlord can refuse consent on any ground whatsoever unless the court's consent is obtained under the compensation procedure of the 1927 Act, or the court orders modification of the lease to enable compliance	If the alteration is an improvement (from the tenant's point of view), the landlord's consent cannot be unreasonably withheld. As a condition for giving consent, the landlord can require a reasonable sum for damage or

		diminution to the value of premises or the landlord's neighbouring premises and proper legal and other expenses. The tenant can be required to undertake to reinstate on termination where this is reasonable and the improvement does not add to the letting value (s 19(2) of the 1927 Act).
User	The landlord can refuse consent on any ground whatsoever.	The landlord can refuse consent on any ground whatsoever unless the lease expressly states to the contrary. A fine cannot be required for giving consent except where structural alterations are involved. This does not preclude the landlord from requiring a reasonable sum and expenses as with a qualified covenant against alterations (s 19(3) of the 1927 Act).

★ The only qualification to the operation of an absolute covenant is where the landlord's objection to a proposed dealing is on the basis of racial or sexual discrimination against the proposed assignee or sub-tenant, or is discrimination based on the disability of that person. In such cases, the covenant will be regarded as fully qualified.

8.1.2 Application to court for declaration

Where consent appears to have been refused unreasonably, the best approach is to apply to the county court for a declaration that the consent has been unreasonably withheld and the dealing, improvement or change of use can proceed without it. The application should set out sufficient particulars to show the grounds on which the applicant claims to be entitled to the declaration sought. A respondent who wishes to oppose the application or to dispute an assertion which it contains must, within 14 days after service of the application on him, file an answer with as many copies as there are other parties to the proceedings. There is no special form provided for such application or answer. It is generally inadvisable for the tenant to proceed without a declaration. The tenant may have interpreted the law incorrectly and have to face forfeiture proceedings to resolve the matter.

8.2 Assignment and sub-letting

8.2.1 Seeking consent

The landlord's consent will not be needed where the lease is silent with regard to assignment and sub-letting. Where the restriction is absolute, the tenant is not precluded from seeking consent, but must comply with the landlord's terms, however unreasonable. Most commonly, the restriction is qualified and the landlord's consent or licence will be required.

The tenant will apply for consent (not the prospective assignee or sub-tenant), usually via an agent such as a solicitor or surveyor submitting to the landlord or its agent a bank reference and two trade references relating to the assignee or sub-tenant. It is often sensible to provide three years' audited accounts in relation to an assignee which is a limited company, as the landlord will almost invariably wish to see these. The request for the bank reference should be made direct by one bank (commonly the assignor's solicitor's bank) to the assignee's bank. Ideally, the letter requesting the reference should contain details of the financial burden to be faced by the assignee by stating the length of the term, the premium, the rent and whether any rent review is pending and the anticipated cost of the works of conversion or fitting out, or to rectify dilapidations. It is good practice to send this letter to the landlord with the reference. The ideal references will be unqualified and explain why the assignee is suitable.

The landlord can ask for whatever information is reasonable to enable it to ascertain whether the assignee or sub-tenant is suitable, such as, in appropriate cases, accounts and profit projections.

Often, an agreement to assign (or sometimes sub-let) will be entered into conditionally upon consent being obtained (see SC 8.3.4).

8.2.2 Statutory restrictions on qualified covenants

The Landlord and Tenant Act 1927. Section 19 of the 1927 Act provides that, notwithstanding any provision to the contrary, the landlord's consent cannot be unreasonably withheld (as to reasonableness, see 8.2.3).

The Landlord and Tenant Act 1988. The 1988 Act has placed tenants in a much stronger position than hitherto. It has not, however, changed the test of reasonableness (*Air India v Balabel* [1993] 30 EG 90). It applies to any tenancy containing a qualified covenant against assigning, sub-letting, charging or parting with possession. A landlord served with a written request for consent to a dealing must, within a reasonable time, give consent in writing (unless it is reasonable to withhold it), stating any conditions to which consent is subject and reasons (where relevant) for withholding consent (s 1(2)). The onus is upon the landlord to show that he has acted reasonably with regard to time, refusing consent or imposing conditions (s 1(6)). Once a reasonable time has elapsed, the landlord cannot raise objections to the assignment or sub-letting which he has not previously raised (*Footwear Corp Ltd v Amplight Properties Ltd* [1998] 3 All ER 52; *Norwich Union Life Assurance Society v Shopmoor Ltd* [1998] All ER 32). What is a reasonable time is a matter for the court. In *Midland Bank plc v Chart Enterprises* [1990] 45 EG 68, a delay of two and a half months in replying to an application was held to be unreasonable. A related issue is when time begins to run (see *Dong Bang Minerva (UK) Ltd v Davina Ltd* [1996] 31 EG 87).

Where a superior landlord's consent is also required and may not be unreasonably withheld, the same obligations extend to the superior landlord (s 3). A claim for breach of statutory duty can be made where a person is in breach of its obligations under the Act (s 4). Service of applications or notices under the 1988 Act are as provided in the lease or, where there is no such provision, as provided by s 23 of the 1927 Act (personal service, or left at, or sent by, registered post or recorded delivery to the last known place of abode in England or Wales and, in the case of a notice to a landlord, the person on whom service may be effected includes any duly authorised agent of the landlord).

On the assignment of a new tenancy, the provisions of the 1988 Act have effect subject to the provisions of the new s 19(1A) of the 1927 Act: see 3.1.7.

Where the lease contains a proviso that, before seeking consent, the tenant must first offer to surrender, the tenant must go through the ritual of offering to surrender. If the landlord accepts, the agreement to surrender is void where the 1954 Act applies to the tenancy (s 38(1)). The tenant then may seek consent in the normal way (*Allnatt London Properties Ltd v Newton* [1984] 1 All ER 423). However, the precise wording of the 'offer back' provisions should be carefully checked in all cases: a well drafted clause may prevent an assignment unless the landlord has specifically rejected the offer to surrender.

The Landlord and Tenant (Covenants) Act 1995. In old leases (that is, those granted before 1 January 1996), the parties could not stipulate in advance what was to be regarded as a reasonable ground for the landlord's refusal of consent to an assignment, the justification being that reasonableness was a matter to be determined objectively. Thus, as regards old tenancies, there is no automatic right for the landlord to insist upon guarantors or upon the proposed assignee or sub-tenant joining in the licence to covenant direct with the landlord, even where the lease purports to make these conditions for the giving of consent. New tenancies, however, may specify any circumstances in which the landlord may withhold his licence or consent to an assignment, or any conditions subject to which any such licence or consent may be granted (see 3.1.7). Such circumstances and conditions will not be tested for reasonableness (provided that they are objective tests, or are applied by the landlord acting reasonably, or are applied by an independent third party). One condition which will be imposed in nearly all cases is that the assignor should enter into an Authorised Guarantee Agreement (see 3.1.3). It should be noted that the new provisions apply only to an assignment, and not to a sub-letting (or charging) of the property.

8.2.3 Reasonableness

In *International Drilling Fluids Ltd v Louisville Investments (Uxbridge) Ltd* [1986] 2 WLR 581, the main principles governing whether a refusal is unreasonable were reiterated. The same principles apply where the transaction for which consent is required is a sub-letting as opposed to an assignment. This will still be good case law in relation to old tenancies (see 3.1.2) and to any conditions or circumstances imposed by the landlord under a new tenancy to which a test of reasonableness applies (see 3.1.7). Reasonableness is judged as at the time of the landlord's decision (*CIN Properties Ltd v Gill* [1993] 38 EG 152).

The Court of Appeal set out the following propositions:

- The purpose of a fully qualified covenant against assignment is to protect the landlord from having his premises used or occupied in an undesirable way or by an undesirable assignee.

- As a corollary to the above proposition, a landlord is not entitled to refuse his consent to an assignment on grounds which have nothing to do with the relationship of landlord and tenant with regard to the subject matter of the lease. For example, it would not be a valid reason that the landlord does not want another service user, but wants to force a change to a more profitable user. A landlord will sometimes refuse consent because the premises are dilapidated. However, this will generally only be relevant (except in serious cases) where evidence is unavailable to show that the prospective assignee is ready, able and willing to put the property in repair within a reasonable time (*Orlando Investments Ltd v Grosvenor Estate Belgravia* [1988] 49 EG 85).

- *The onus of proving that consent has been unreasonably withheld is on the tenant.* As noted above, this has since been overturned by the Landlord and Tenant Act 1988, which applies to all leases (whether entered into before or after the Act came into force on 29 September 1988) and obliges the landlord to show that his refusal was reasonable (s 1(6)(c)).

- *It is not necessary for the landlord to prove that the conclusions which led him to refuse consent were justified, if they were conclusions which might be reached by a reasonable man in the circumstances.*

- *It may be reasonable for the landlord to refuse his consent to an assignment on the ground of the purpose for which the proposed assignee intends to use the premises even though that purpose is not forbidden by the lease.* By contrast, the landlord has no right to refuse consent solely on the basis of a potential breach of user covenant because the covenant may still be enforced against the assignee (*Ashworth Frazer Ltd v Gloucester CC* (2000) 80 P&CR 11).

- *A landlord need normally only consider his own relevant interests when deciding whether to refuse or give consent, but there may be cases where there is such a disproportion between the benefit to the landlord and the detriment to the tenant if the landlord refuses consent that it is unreasonable for the landlord to refuse consent.*

- *Subject to the above propositions it is a question of fact in each case depending on all the circumstances whether the landlord's consent is being unreasonably withheld.*

In *Mount Eden Land Ltd v Straudley Investments Ltd* (1996) 74 P&CR 306, Phillips LJ suggested that two further propositions might be added to those set out in *International Drilling Fluids*:

• it will normally be considered reasonable for a landlord to refuse consent or impose a condition if this is necessary to prevent his contractual rights under the head lease being prejudiced by the proposed assignment or sub-lease;

• it will normally be considered unreasonable for the landlord to seek to impose a condition which would increase or enhance the control which the landlord was able to exercise under the terms of the head lease.

8.2.4 Drafting the licence

(See Precedent 9.4.) Often, the landlord's solicitor will write to the tenant's solicitor stating that, before any work is done, the tenant's solicitor must undertake to be responsible for the landlord's costs. The tenant's solicitor should only give an undertaking to pay the landlord's reasonable costs after agreeing a maximum figure with the landlord's solicitor with the authorisation of the tenant and (if this can be achieved without embarrassment) after obtaining sufficient money from the tenant on account to cover this figure. Alternatively, the tenant's solicitor should politely decline, again agreeing a maximum figure and confirming, with the tenant's authority, that the tenant will be responsible for reasonable fees up to that figure.

The landlord's solicitor will prepare a draft deed giving consent and will send it in duplicate to the tenant's solicitor who will in turn forward it to the assignee's solicitor. Where appropriate on the assignment of a new tenancy, the landlord's solicitor will also prepare a draft AGA. This may either be in a separate deed, or contained in the licence to assign. Once approved by all relevant parties, an engrossment of the licence will be prepared by the landlord's solicitor. One copy will be executed by the tenant and one by the landlord and the parts exchanged, so that the tenant has the landlord's executed part and vice versa. If, as the landlord under an old tenancy usually requires, the assignee is to enter into direct covenants with the landlord, then the licence will be in three parts (under a new tenancy, direct covenants are unnecessary – see 3.1.8). Sometimes, all three parts (or two, as the case may be) will be executed by each party. When the licence has been completed, each party will hold one part.

In the licence, the landlord will consent to the assignment or sub-letting and the tenant will, among other things, covenant to pay the landlord's costs. On the assignment of an old tenancy, the assignee will usually be required to covenant to observe the covenants in the lease. Without such a covenant, an assignee is liable only up until it disposes of its own interest and it should try to resist entering into a covenant in the terms required by the landlord. It is undecided whether such a requirement is justified in the context of an assignment. On the assignment of a new tenancy, such a direct covenant is unnecessary. Similarly, a sub-tenant is not liable to a superior landlord and such a landlord may try to avoid this problem by requiring direct covenants in the licence to underlet. In the post-1988 Act climate, tenants should be more ready to challenge landlord's requirements without being so concerned about possible delay.

8.3 Alterations

8.3.1 Seeking consent

If the lease does not expressly forbid the proposed alterations, the tenant does not need to seek the landlord's consent (subject to the doctrine of waste). If the alterations are absolutely forbidden, the tenant can seek consent, which may be refused, however unreasonably.

Whether the restriction on alterations is absolute or qualified, the tenant may obtain the court's consent under the compensation procedures of the 1927 Act (see 2.3), or otherwise make application to the court where legislation allows the court to modify the lease to enable the tenant to comply with statutory obligations such as those imposed by the Fire Precautions Act 1971 (see Aldridge, *Letting Business Premises,* 7th edn, 1996, London: Sweet & Maxwell).

Where there is a qualified covenant precluding alterations except with the landlord's consent then, with regard to improvements, there is an implied reasonableness proviso extending to refusal or consent subject to permitted conditions. The availability of such conditions means that the landlord will rarely be able simply to refuse consent to improvements outright, and the issue will often turn on the reasonableness of the conditions.

The landlord should require the fullest possible information with regard to the proposed alterations, including plans and evidence of planning, building regulations and other appropriate consents and approvals.

8.3.2 Drafting the licence

A draft deed granting consent is prepared by the landlord's solicitor and submitted in duplicate to the tenant's solicitor. When approved, it will be engrossed in duplicate. Generally, one part will be executed by the tenant and one by the landlord. Both parts will be exchanged, so that the tenant has the licence executed by the landlord, and the landlord the counterpart executed by the tenant.

The main drafting issues are: first, what conditions the landlord should impose and the tenant accept; and, secondly, whether the tenant should be placed under an obligation to carry out the works.

Although the landlord can require the payment of money or reinstatement at the end of the lease, the tenant is obliged to accept such conditions only if they are reasonable. The landlord should consider a reinstatement provision where the alterations are of benefit only to the tenant. Where the improvements add to the letting value, the tenant can resist a reinstatement condition and thereby preserve his rights to compensation under the 1927 Act. Compensation must not exceed the net addition to the value of the premises and if the reinstatement takes place, there will be no such addition. Where a reinstatement condition is inserted, the landlord should consider attaching both 'before' and 'after' plans. Such plans will also be good evidence for determining the rent on review and statutory renewal under the 1954 Act where improvements are to be disregarded.

Imposing an obligation upon the tenant to execute the works has certain advantages so far as the landlord is concerned.

First, s 2(1) of the 1927 Act provides that compensation is unavailable for improvements carried out by the tenant pursuant to a contract for valuable consideration. Such consideration includes a rent-free period, a payment of money to the tenant exceeding a nominal figure (but not necessarily representing full compensation), or possibly even waiving the benefit of an absolute bar on alterations.

Secondly, s 34 of the 1954 Act stipulates that only a tenant's voluntary improvements should be disregarded in determining the rent on renewal of the lease pursuant to the Act and most rent review clauses are drafted to similar effect. It is extremely disadvantageous to the tenant to pay the actual cost of the improvements and then to have to pay a higher rent, in consequence, on renewal or review.

Care must be taken with regard to drafting. A landlord will wish to require the tenant, amongst other things, to execute the works pursuant to planning and building regulations and other statutory consents and in a good and workmanlike manner. However, the tenant will usually still have the choice whether to carry out the works in the first instance and there will, in such a case, be no obligation involved (*Godbold v Martin the Newsagents Ltd* [1983] 268 EG 1202). Ideally, the licence should expressly state whether or not the tenant is under such an obligation.

8.4 User

8.4.1 Seeking consent

The lease may include a covenant imposing an absolute restriction on the tenant against changing the use from any stated user defined by the lease. In such a case, the landlord cannot be compelled to permit a change of use, even if his attitude is completely unreasonable. A change may be agreed in subsequent negotiations and should be effected by a deed of variation. Such a covenant is likely to have an adverse effect on any rent review, therefore it is more common in commercial leases for the covenant to be qualified, requiring the landlord's consent before the use can be changed.

Whether the covenant restricting the user is absolute or permits a change with the landlord's consent, the landlord can refuse consent or impose onerous conditions without constraint save that, where the covenant is qualified, a fine can be required only where the change involves structural alterations. Generally, a landlord need act reasonably only where a qualified covenant expressly requires it not to refuse consent unreasonably (although note that the landlord can, in some circumstances, require a 'reasonable sum'). The circumstances justifying a refusal of consent where there is a reasonableness proviso are similar to those where a landlord can refuse consent reasonably to an assignment or sub-letting.

In addition to the stated user clause, there may be a covenant requiring the tenant to comply with planning law or, alternatively, prohibiting the tenant from making any application for planning permission.

8.4.2 Drafting the licence

The procedure involved is similar to that where there is a licence permitting alterations. Where the covenant is absolute, the licence may take the form of a deed varying the user clause. The landlord's solicitor should make consent conditional upon the tenant obtaining planning permission and any other appropriate consents, and should also carefully consider the rent review implications. The lease may need to be varied so that the rent on review is the higher of the rental values where the premises are, first, let for the existing user and, secondly, for the new user. However, the amended user clause should then provide that it will be assumed (where appropriate) that the premises have been physically adapted and may lawfully be used for the existing user. Failure to provide such express assumptions may have a depreciatory effect on the rental value of the existing user once planning permission has been obtained and alterations made in connection with the new user. This will be a costly mistake if the new user commands a lower rental value.

9 Precedents

9.1 Tenancy at will

THIS AGREEMENT is made on *the first day of May 2000*

BETWEEN *A Limited* whose registered office is *1 High Street, Worktown* ('the Landlord') of the one part and *B Limited* whose registered office is *10 Sea Road, Durton on Sea* ('the Tenant') of the other part

WHEREAS:

1 The Landlord intends ultimately to carry out certain alterations to the premises demised by this agreement and in the meantime wishes to let the premises on a temporary basis

2 The Tenant wishes to occupy the premises temporarily for the purposes of its business of the sale of fruit and vegetables

3 The Landlord wishes to grant and the Tenant wishes to take a tenancy at will of the premises

IT IS AGREED as follows

1 The Landlord lets and the Tenant takes the premises known as 10 High Street Worktown ('the Premises') on a tenancy at will commencing on the seventh day of May 2000

2 The Tenant will pay a rent calculated at the rate of Twenty pounds (£20.00) per day whenever the Landlord shall demand it provided that neither the payment of rent at regular intervals nor any demand for payment of it nor the subsequent calculation of rent by reference to a period is to create or cause the tenancy to become a periodic tenancy

3   The Tenant agrees with the Landlord:

  (a) To pay the rent without deduction or set off when demanded

  (b) To pay and indemnify the Landlord against all taxes outgoings charges and rates payable in respect of the Premises during the currency of the tenancy

  (c) Not to make any alterations or additions to the Premises

  (d) To keep the Premises in the same state of repair and decorative condition as existed on the commencement date of this tenancy as evidenced in the Schedule of Condition annexed to this agreement

  (e) Not to assign underlet charge share or otherwise part with possession of the Premises or any part thereof

  (f) Not to use the Premises or any part of the Premises otherwise than for the sale of fruit and vegetables

  (g) Not to cause any nuisance or annoyance to the Landlord or to the owner or occupier of any neighbouring premises

  (h) To permit the Landlord and all persons authorised by the Landlord to enter the Premises on giving twenty-four hours' notice or at any time in an emergency to inspect or carry out works to the Premises or any neighbouring premises

This document is executed as a Deed on the date stated at the beginning of this Deed

EXECUTED AS A DEED BY A LIMITED

in the presence of:

Director

Secretary

EXECUTED AS A DEED BY B LIMITED

in the presence of:

Director

Secretary

Commentary

A tenancy at will is not protected by Pt II of the Landlord and Tenant Act 1954 and can be brought to an end at any time by either party without any need for a break clause or proviso for forfeiture. Recitals should be included explaining the circumstances in which the tenancy at will has been granted as it must be shown to be genuine. Care must be taken not to create a periodic tenancy; this has been achieved here by creating a daily rent. Such a tenancy should only be used on a short term basis, because regular payments of rent with reference to a period may give rise to the implication of a periodic tenancy. It is fatal to a tenancy at will to include a period of notice on which the tenancy can be determined.

Given the nature of a tenancy at will, it is unlikely that the tenant will prepared to take on obligations which are any more onerous than those included above.

9.2 Forms in connection with a joint application to the county court for an order under Pt II, s 38(4) of the Landlord and Tenant Act 1954

9.2.1 Claim form (CPR Pt 8)

IN THE **Worktown** COUNTY COURT   Claim no

(Landlord) *Walter Smith*   First Claimant

– and –

(Tenant) *X Limited*   Second Claimant

JOINT APPLICATION PURSUANT TO s 38(4) OF THE LANDLORD AND TENANT ACT 1954 AS AMENDED BY THE LAW OF PROPERTY ACT 1969

Details of Claim

1   The claim is a Part 8 Section B claim as the Claimants are seeking the Court's decision on a question which does not involve a substantial dispute of fact and the Claim is one which would have been brought by originating application before 26 April 1999.

2   The above-named First Claimant of 44 The Avenue Newtown HEREBY APPLIES to the Court jointly with the Second Claimant whose registered office is at The Grange Worktown for an Order pursuant to s 38(4) of the Landlord and Tenant Act 1954 Part II (as amended by s 5 of the Law of Property Act) authorising an agreement excluding the provisions of ss 24 to 28 (inclusive) of the said Act in relation to a tenancy of premises known as 45 High Street Worktown ('the premises') intended to be created by a Lease to be made between the First Claimant as Landlord and the Second Applicant as Tenant.

3   The agreed form of Lease is attached to this Application.

4   The grounds upon which the First Applicant and the Second Applicant claim to be entitled to the Order are

(a) a settled draft of the proposed Lease is attached to this Application and as appears from clause ... the First Claimant is to grant a tenancy of the premises to the Second Claimant for a term of ... years

Second Claimant's name and address

X Limited
The Grange
Worktown

Court fee **£120**

Solicitor's costs –

Issue date

Details of claim (continued)

(a) it is a term of the negotiations for the grant of the proposed Lease that the occupation of the premises by the Second Claimant shall not be protected by ss 24–28 of the said Act as appears from clause … of the annexed draft of the proposed Lease

(b) the First Claimant intends to redevelop the Premises or is likely to require them for redevelopment

(c) exclusion of the Second Claimant's rights has been taken into account when negotiating the length of term granted and the rent reserved by the proposed Lease.

1   The Second Claimant has received legal advice independently from the First Claimant and is aware of the rights which it would otherwise have under the Act but in the circumstances mentioned above considers it reasonable to forgo such rights and has therefore agreed to enter into the proposed Lease in the form of the draft annexed hereto

2   Notwithstanding the location of the premises the First Claimant and the Second Claimant have agreed to be subject to the jurisdiction of this Court and an application is made that these proceedings be decided by this Court pursuant to CPR Part 30.2.]

3   It is not intended to serve this Application on any other person

Statement of Truth

★(I believe) (The First Claimant believes) that the facts stated in these particulars of claim are true.

★I am duly authorised by the claimant to sign this statement.

Full name ....

Name of First Claimant's solicitors' firm **A Solicitor and Co**

Signed position or office held

★(Claimant) (Claimant's solicitor) (if signing on behalf of firm or company)

★ delete as appropriate

Statement of Truth

★(I believe) (The Second Claimant believes) that the facts stated in these particulars of claim are true.

*I am duly authorised by the claimant to sign this statement.

Full name ....

Name of Second Claimant's solicitors' firm *Hopitees*

Signed position or office held

*(Claimant) (Claimant's solicitor) (if signing on behalf of firm or company)

* delete as appropriate

First Claimant's solicitors' address to which documents should be sent if different from overleaf. If you are prepared to accept delivery by DX, fax or e-mail, please add details:

23 High Street
Worktown

Second Claimant's solicitors' address to which documents should be sent if different from overleaf. If you are prepared to accept delivery by DX, fax or e-mail, please add details:

The Towers
Worktown

9.2.2 County Court Order excluding the 1954 Act

IN THE WORKTOWN COUNTY COURT

Claim no:

In the Matter of the Landlord and Tenant Act 1954 and

In the Matter of a Proposed Lease of the Premises

known as *45 High Street Worktown*

BETWEEN

(Landlord) *Walter Smith*   First Claimant

– and –

(Tenant) *X Limited*   Second Claimant

CONSENT ORDER

UPON THE JOINT APPLICATION of the First Claimant and the Second Claimant and it appearing that the Claimants jointly apply for the relief sought by this application and by their respective solicitors have consented in writing to this Order

IT IS ORDERED pursuant to s 38(4) of the Landlord and Tenant Act 1954 that the Claimants be at liberty to enter into an agreement excluding the provisions of ss 24 to 28 inclusive of the said Landlord and Tenant Act 1954 in relation to the intended tenancy to the Second Claimant such agreement to be in the terms contained in the said intended tenancy agreement a draft whereof is attached to this Order and signed by the District Judge

Dated this   day of   2001

DISTRICT JUDGE

Commentary

While the wording of the draft order, which always has to be submitted to the court, is effectively unchanged, the application form has been substituted by a Pt 8 Claim Form.

Paragraph B6 of the second Practice Direction to CPR Pt 8 requires the exclusion application to be made only to the court where one of the applicants lives or carries on business or where the property in question is situated. The claim form above incorporates a jurisdiction clause acknowledging that the premises are not within the geographical jurisdiction of the court, confirming that the claimants have agreed to be subject to the jurisdiction of the court and requesting that the proceedings be decided by the court pursuant to CPR, Pt 30.2 (the rule allowing applications to be made at the 'wrong court'). If the property does fall within the jurisdiction of the court this clause may, of course, be deleted. It should be borne in mind, however, that there is no provision which allows parties to agree to another court being used for applications of this kind. In practice, some judges will rely on the parties' consent while others will not. Orders made by the 'wrong' court may well be treated as effective by the assumption that the court applied r 30.2(2)(b) or r 3.10(b).

The court has a discretion to refuse an application and the parties should set out grounds, not merely rely on stating 'the parties are in agreement'.

The application should always state that the parties have been advised of the effect of the exclusion of the provisions of ss 24–28 of the Landlord and Tenant Act 1954. However, there is no binding requirement that parties to a s 38(4) application are advised by solicitors. Where the parties are unrepresented, therefore, a paragraph is commonly added to an application to the court to reflect the fact that the parties are unrepresented:

> The Second Claimant has had an opportunity to take legal advice on the effect of the Order sought but has decided to forgo his rights under the Landlord and Tenant Act 1954 and both Claimants are willing to make this application.

In such a situation, it is also advisable for the landlord to make the tenant sign a letter to the effect that the tenant is aware of the exclusion of ss 24–28 of the Landlord and Tenant Act 1954.

The claimants (normally via the landlord's solicitor) will file:

- self-addressed envelopes where the application is made through the post;
- a request for issue of the application;
- a Pt 8 Claim Form and two copies with the agreed form of lease attached;
- a draft court order signed by both parties' solicitors containing a statement that 'We hereby consent to an order in these terms' and (as a matter of courtesy) three further copies without such a statement for use by the court;

• a cheque for £120.

The application may be heard and determined by the district judge in chambers (CCR Ord 43, r 15(2)). It is unusual for either party to attend at court and the application is normally dealt with through the post.

The agreement is usually contained in a proviso in the lease (see 6.9.6).

9.3 Statutory renewal forms

Examples are given of the following:

(a) landlord's notice for particulars;

(b) tenant's notice for particulars;

(c) landlord's s 25 notice;

(d) tenant's counter-notice;

(e) tenant's s 26 request;

(f) landlord's counter-notice;

(g) tenant's claim for new tenancy;

(h) landlord's answer;

(i) notice of discontinuance;

(j) consent order dismissing tenants' application for a new lease.

It should be noted that (e) and (f) are alternatives to (c) and (d). Which is relevant depends upon whether the landlord or the tenant is the first to initiate the 1954 Act procedure by serving a s 25 notice or a s 26 request respectively. The advantage often lies with whoever serves the notice or request (see 4.5). Thus, if the landlord has delayed serving a s 25 notice, this would enable the tenant to extend his tenancy by serving a s 26 request for a new tenancy 12 months hence (but only before the landlord has served a s 25 notice).

9.3.1 Notice by landlord requiring information about occupation and sub-tenancies of business premises

LANDLORD AND TENANT ACT 1954
SECTION 40(1)

To: [name of tenant]

Of: [address of tenant]

> Important – This notice requires you to give your landlord certain information. You must act quickly. Read the notice and all the notes carefully. If you are in any doubt about the action you should take, get advice immediately eg from a solicitor or surveyor or a citizens advice bureau.

1   This notice is given under s 40(1) of the Landlord and Tenant Act 1954.

2   It relates to [description of property] of which you are the tenant.

3   I/We require you to notify me/us in writing, within one month of the service of this notice on you:

   (a) whether you occupy the premises or any part of them wholly or partly for business purposes; and

   (b) whether you have a sub-tenant.

4   If you have a sub-tenant, I/we also require you to state:

   (a) what premises are comprised in the sub-tenancy

   (b) if the sub-tenancy is for a fixed term what the term is, or, if the sub-tenancy is terminable by notice, by what notice it can be terminated;

   (c) what rent the sub-tenant pays;

   (d) the sub-tenant's full name;

   (e) whether, to the best of your knowledge and belief, the sub-tenant occupies either the whole or part of the premises sub-let to him and, if not, what is his address.

5   All correspondence about this notice should be sent to [the landlord] [the landlord's agent] at the address given below.

Date

Signature of [landlord][the landlord's agent]

Name of landlord

Address of landlord

[Address of agent]

NOTES

Purpose of this notice

1 Your landlord (or, if he is a tenant himself, possibly his landlord) has served this notice on you to obtain the information he needs in order to find out his position under Part II of the Landlord and Tenant Act 1954 in relation to your tenancy. He will then know, for example, whether, when your tenancy expires, you will be entitled to apply to the court for a new tenancy of the whole of the premises comprised in your present tenancy; you may not be entitled to a new tenancy of any part of the premises which you have sub-let. (In certain circumstances, a sub-tenant may become a direct tenant of the landlord.)

Replying to this notice

2 Section 40 of the 1954 Act says that you must answer the questions asked in the notice and you must let the landlord have your answers in writing within one month of the service of the notice. You do not need a special form for this. If you do not answer these questions or give the landlord incorrect information he might suffer a loss for which, in certain circumstances, you could be held liable.

3 If you have let to more than one sub-tenant you should give the information required in respect of each sub-letting.

Validity of this notice

4 The landlord who has given this notice may not be the landlord to whom you pay your rent. 'Business' is given a wide meaning in the 1954 Act and is used in the same sense in this notice. The landlord cannot ask for this information earlier than two years before your tenancy is due to expire or could be brought to an end by notice given by him. If you have any doubts about whether this notice is valid, get immediate advice.

Explanatory booklet

5 The Department of the Environment and Welsh Office booklet *Business Leases and Security of Tenure* explains the main provisions of Part II of the 1954 Act. It is available from the Department of the Environment Publications Store, Building No 3, Victoria Road, South Ruislip, Middlesex.

9.3.2 Notice by tenant of business premises requiring information from landlord about landlord's interest

LANDLORD AND TENANT ACT 1954
SECTION 40(2)

To: [name of tenant]

Of: [address of tenant]

Important – This notice requires you to give your tenant certain information. You must act quickly. Read the notice and all the notes carefully. If you are in any doubt about the action you should take, get advice immediately eg from a solicitor or surveyor or a citizens advice bureau.

---

1   This notice is given under s 40(2) of the Landlord and Tenant Act 1954.

2   It relates to [description of property] of which you are the landlord.

3   I/We give you notice requiring you to notify me/us in writing, within one month of the service of this notice on you:

(a) whether you are the freeholder of the whole or part of the premises.

If you are *not* the freeholder:

(b) I/We also require you to state, to the best of your knowledge and belief:

(i)   the name and address of the person who is your immediate landlord in respect of the premises or the part of which you are not the freeholder;

(ii)   the length of your tenancy; and

(iii) the earliest date (if any) at which your tenancy can be terminated by notice to quit given by your immediate landlord.

4   I/We also require you to notify me/us:

(a) whether there is a mortgagee in possession of your interest in the property and, if so, his name and address; and

(b) if there is a receiver appointed by the mortgagee or by the court, his name and address also.

5   All correspondence about this notice should be sent to [the tenant] [the tenant's agent] at the address given below.

Date

Signature of [tenant] [tenant's agent]

Name of tenant

Address of tenant

[Address of agent]

NOTES

Purpose of this notice

1   Your tenant has served this notice on you to obtain the information he needs in order to find out who is his landlord for the purposes of Part II of the Landlord and Tenant Act 1954. The Act in certain circumstances enables a tenant of business premises to obtain a new tenancy from that landlord.

Replying to this notice

2   Section 40 of the 1954 Act says that you must answer the questions asked in the notice and you must let your tenant have your answers in writing within one month of the service of the notice. You do not need a special form for this. If you do not answer these questions or give your tenant incorrect information he might suffer a loss for which, in certain circumstances, you could be held liable.

Validity of this notice

3   'Business' is given a wide meaning in the 1954 Act and is used in the same sense in this notice. Your tenant cannot ask for this information earlier than two years before his current tenancy is due to expire or could be brought to an end by notice to quit given by you. If you have any doubts about whether this notice is valid, get immediate advice.

Explanatory booklet

4   [The Department of the Environment and Welsh Office booklet *Business Leases and Security of Tenure* explains the main provisions of Part II of the 1954 Act. It is available from the Department of the Environment Publications Store, Building No 3, Victoria Road, South Ruislip, Middlesex.]

9.3.3 Landlord's s 25 notice

Care should be taken in preparing the s 25 notice, as mistakes can render it invalid. For example, if the landlord's name and address are inaccurate, the notice itself will be ineffective (see *Morrow v Nadeem* [1086] 1 WLR 1381). If a mistake is noticed in time, the landlord may withdraw the first invalid notice and replace it with a valid one (*Smith v Draper* [1990] 2 EGLR 69).

LANDLORD AND TENANT ACT 1954
SECTION 25

Landlord's Notice to Terminate Business Tenancy

To   **O Limited**

of   **22 High Row, Marton on Tyne, Northumberland**

Important – This notice is intended to bring your tenancy to an end. If you want to continue to occupy your property you must act quickly. Read the notice and all the notes carefully. If you are in any doubt about the action you should take, get advice immediately eg from a solicitor or surveyor or a citizens advice bureau.

---

1   This notice is given under s 25 of the Landlord and Tenant Act 1954.

2   It relates to **the premises known as 22 High Row, Marton on Tyne** of which you are the tenant.

3   I/We give you notice terminating your tenancy on **5 July 2001**.

4   Within two months after the giving of this notice, you must notify me/us in writing whether or not you are willing to give up possession of the property comprised in the tenancy on the date stated in para 3.

[5   If you apply to the court under Part II of the Landlord and Tenant Act 1954 for the grant of a new tenancy, I/we will not oppose your application.]

OR

[5   If you apply to the court under Part II of the Landlord and Tenant Act 1954 for the grant of a new tenancy, I/we will oppose it on the grounds mentioned in paragraph(s) (f) of s 30(1) of the Act.]

6.   All correspondence about this notice should be sent to (8) [the landlord] [the landlord's agent] at the address given below.

Date *1 January 2001*

Signature of ~~[landlord]~~[landlord's agent] *A Solicitor and Co*

Name of landlord *A Limited*

Address of landlord *1 High Street, Worktown*

(8)[Address of agent] *A Solicitor and Co*
23 High Street
Worktown
Northumberland

* This form must NOT be used if:

(a) no previous notice terminating the tenancy has been given under s 25 of the Act, and

(b) the tenancy is the tenancy of a house (as defined for the purposes of Part I of the Leasehold Reform Act 1967), and

(c) the tenancy is a long tenancy at a low rent (within the meaning of that Act of 1967), and

(d) the tenant is not a company or other artificial person.

If the above apply, use form number 13 [Oyez No L&T 24] instead of this form.

NOTES

Termination of tenancy

1   This notice is intended to bring your tenancy to an end. You can apply to the court for a new tenancy under the Landlord and Tenant Act 1954 by following the procedure outlined in notes 2 and 3 below. If you do, your tenancy will continue after the date shown in para 3 of this notice while your claim is being considered. The landlord can ask the court to fix the rent, which you will have to pay while the tenancy continues. The terms of any new tenancy not agreed between you and the landlord will be settled by the court.

Claiming a new tenancy

2   If you want to apply to the court for a new tenancy you must:

(1) notify the landlord in writing not later than two months after the giving of this notice that you are not willing to give up possession of the property [Oyez No L&T 25A];

AND

(2) apply to the court, not earlier than two months nor later than four months after the giving of this notice, for a new tenancy.

3   The time limits in note 2 run from the giving of the notice. The date of the giving of the notice may not be the date written on the notice or the date on which you actually saw it. It may, for instance, be the date on which the notice was delivered through the post to your last address known to the person giving the notice. If there has been any delay in your seeing this notice, you may need to act very quickly. If you are in any doubt, get advice immediately.

WARNING TO TENANT

If you do not keep to the time limits in Note 2, you
will lose your right to apply to the court for a new tenancy.

Landlord's opposition to claim for a new tenancy

4   If you apply to the court for a new tenancy, the landlord can only oppose your application on one or more of the grounds set out in s 30(1) of the 1954 Act. These grounds are set out below. The paragraph letters are those given in the Act. The landlord can only use a ground if its paragraph letter is shown in para 5 of the notice.

Grounds

(a) where under the current tenancy the tenant has any obligations as respects the repair and maintenance of the holding, that the tenant ought not to be granted a new tenancy in view of the state of repair of the holding, being a state resulting from the tenant's failure to comply with the said obligations;

(b) that the tenant ought not to be granted a new tenancy in view of his persistent delay in paying rent which has become due;

(c) that the tenant ought not to be granted a new tenancy in view of other substantial breaches by him of his obligations under the current tenancy, or for any other reason connected with the tenant's use or management of the holding;

(d) that the landlord has offered and is willing to provide or secure the provision of alternative accommodation for the tenant, that the terms on which the alternative accommodation is available are reasonable having regard to the terms of the current tenancy and to all other relevant circumstances, and that the accommodation and the time at which it will be available are suitable for the tenant's requirements (including the requirement to preserve goodwill) having regard to the nature and class of his business and to the situation and extent of, and facilities afforded by, the holding;

(e) where the current tenancy was created by the sub-letting of part only of the property comprised in a superior tenancy and the landlord is the owner of an interest in reversion expectant on the termination of that superior tenancy, that the aggregate of the rents reasonably obtainable on separate lettings of the holding and the remainder of that property would be substantially less than the rent reasonably obtainable on a letting of that property as a whole, that on the termination of the current tenancy the landlord requires possession of the holding for the purposes of letting or otherwise disposing of the said property as a whole, and that in view thereof the tenant ought not to be granted a new tenancy;

(f) that on the termination of the current tenancy the landlord intends to demolish or reconstruct the premises comprised in the holding or a substantial part of those premises or to carry out substantial work of construction on the holding or part thereof and that he could not reasonably do so without obtaining possession of the holding;

(If the landlord uses this ground, the court can sometimes still grant a new tenancy if certain conditions set out in s 31A of the Act can be met.)

(g) that on the termination of the current tenancy the landlord intends to occupy the holding for the purposes, or partly for the purposes, of a business to be carried on by him therein, or as his residence.

(The landlord must normally have been the landlord for at least five years to use this ground.)

Compensation

5   If you cannot get a new tenancy solely because grounds (e), (f) or (g) apply, you are entitled to compensation under the 1954 Act. If your landlord has opposed your application on any of the other grounds as well as (e), (f) or (g) you can only get compensation if the court's refusal to grant a new tenancy is based solely on grounds (e), (f) or (g). In other words, you cannot get compensation under the 1954 Act if the court has refused your tenancy on other grounds even if (e), (f), (g) also apply.

6   If your landlord is an authority possessing compulsory purchase powers (such as a local authority), you may be entitled to a disturbance payment under Part III of the Land Compensation Act 1973.

Negotiating a new tenancy

7   Most leases are renewed by negotiation. If you do try to agree a new tenancy with your landlord, remember:

(1) that your present tenancy will not be extended after the date in para 3 of this notice unless you both

(a)   give written notice that you will not vacate (note 2(1) above); and

(b)   apply to the court for a new tenancy (note 2(2) above);

that you will lose your right to apply to the court if you do not keep to the time limits in note 2.

Validity of this notice

8   The landlord who has given this notice may not be the landlord to whom you pay your rent. 'Business' is given a wide meaning in the 1954 Act and is used in the same sense in this notice. The 1954 Act also has rules about the date which the landlord can put in para 3. This depends on the terms of your tenancy. If you have any doubts about whether this notice is valid, get immediate advice.

Explanatory booklet

9   The Department of the Environment and Welsh Office booklet *Business Leases and Security of Tenure* explains the main provisions of Part II of the 1954 Act. It is available from The Department of the Environment Publications Store, Building No 3, Victoria Road, South Ruislip, Middlesex.

9.3.4 Tenant's counter-notice

LANDLORD AND TENANT ACT 1954
SECTIONS 25(5) AND 29(2)

Tenant's Counter-Notice as to Willingness to
Give Up Possession of Business Premises

To   *A Limited*

of   *1 High Street, Worktown, Northumberland*

I/we received on   *2 January 2001* your notice terminating

my/our tenancy of   *22 High Row, Marton on Tyne*

on   *5 July 2001*

TAKE NOTICE that I/we will [not] be willing to give up possession of
the property comprised in the tenancy on that date.

DATED   16 January 2001

Signed: *Hopitees*

[As solicitor/agent for] Tenant

Name of Tenant: *O Limited*

Address of Tenant: *22 High Row, Marton on Tyne,*
                     Northumberland

[Name and address of solicitor/agent]

Hopitees
Solicitors
The Towers
Worktown
Northumberland

NOTES

1   This counter-notice must normally be given to the landlord who
    served the notice terminating the tenancy, who may not be the
    immediate landlord to whom the rent is paid. The identity of the
    landlord to whom the counter-notice has to be given may change:
    see Landlord and Tenant Act 1954, s 44.

2   This counter-notice must be given within two months of the landlord's
    notice being given.

3   The tenant cannot apply to the court for a new tenancy unless a
    counter-notice, stating that he will not be willing to give up possession,
    has been duly given.

9.3.5 Tenant's s 26 request

LANDLORD AND TENANT ACT 1954
SECTION 26

Tenant's Request for New Tenancy of Business Premises

To (1)   *A Limited*

of (2)   *1 High Street, Worktown,
                    Northumberland*

Important – This is a request for a new tenancy of your property
or part of it. If you want to oppose this request you must act
quickly. Read the request and all the notes carefully. If you are in
any doubt about the action you should take, get advice immediately
eg from a solicitor or surveyor or a citizens advice bureau.

---

1   This request is made under s 26 of the Landlord and Tenant Act 1954.

2   You are the landlord of   *22 High Row Marton on Tyne
                                Northumberland*

3   I/We request you to grant a new tenancy beginning on
    30 December 2001

4   I/we propose that:

    (a) the property comprised in the new tenancy should be

         22 High Row, Marton on Tyne, Northumberland.

    (b) the rent payable under the new tenancy should be

         £10,000 per annum.

    (c) the other terms of the new tenancy should be

         *A term of five years with a break clause exercisable
         by either party serving not less than three months'
         notice on the other expiring at the end of the
         third year of the term but otherwise on the same
         terms as the current tenancy.*

5   All correspondence about this request should be sent to [the tenant]
    [the tenant's agent] at the address given below.

Date   *1 January 2001*

Signature of (4) [tenant] [tenant's agent] *Hopitees*

Name of tenant   *O Limited*

Address of tenant   *22 High Row, Marton on Tyne,
                        Northumberland*

[Address of agent]   *Hopitees*
                         Solicitors
                         The Towers
                         Worktown
                         Northumberland

NOTES

Request for a new tenancy

1   This request by your tenant for a new tenancy brings his current tenancy to an end on the day before the date mentioned in para 3 above. He can apply to the court under the Landlord and Tenant Act 1954 for a new tenancy. If he does, his current tenancy will continue after the date mentioned in para 3 of this request while his application is being considered by the court. You can ask the court to fix the rent which your tenant will have to pay whilst his tenancy continues. The terms of any new tenancy not agreed between you and your tenant will be settled by the court.

Opposing a request for a new tenancy

2   If you do not want to grant a new tenancy, you must, within two months of the making of this request, give your tenant notice saying that you will oppose any application he makes to the court for a new tenancy. You do not need a special form to do this, but you must state on which of the grounds set out in the 1954 Act you will oppose the application: see note 4.

3   The time limit in note 2 runs from the making of this request. The date of the making of the request may not be the date written on the request or the date on which you actually saw it. It may, for instance, be the date on which the request was delivered through the post to your last address known to the person giving the request. If there has been any delay in your seeing this request you may need to act very quickly. If you are in any doubt, get advice immediately.

WARNING TO LANDLORD

If you do not keep to the time limit in note 2, you will lose your right to oppose your tenant's application to the court for a new tenancy if he makes one.

Grounds for opposing an application

4   If your tenant applies to the court for a new tenancy, you can only

oppose the application on one or more of the grounds set out in s 30(1) of the 1954 Act. These grounds are set out below. The paragraph letters are those given in the Act.

Grounds

(a) Where under the current tenancy the tenant has any obligations as respects the repair and maintenance of the holding, that the tenant ought not to be granted a new tenancy in view of the state of repair of the holding, being a state resulting from the tenant's failure to comply with the said obligations;

(b) that the tenant ought not to be granted a new tenancy in view of his persistent delay in paying rent which has become due;

(c) that the tenant ought not to be granted a new tenancy in view of other substantial breaches by him of his obligations under the current tenancy, or for any other reason connected with the tenant's use or management of the holding;

(d) that you have offered and are willing to provide or secure the provision of alternative accommodation for the tenant, that the terms on which the alternative accommodation is available are reasonable having regard to the terms of the current tenancy and to all other relevant circumstances, and that the accommodation and the time at which it will be available are suitable for the tenant's requirements (including the requirement to preserve goodwill) having regard to the nature and class of his business and to the situation and extent of, and facilities afforded by, the holding;

(e) where the current tenancy was created by the sub-letting of part only of the property comprised in a superior tenancy and you are the owner of an interest in reversion expectant on the termination of that superior tenancy, that the aggregate of the rents reasonably obtainable on separate lettings of the holding and the remainder of that property would be substantially less than the rent reasonably obtainable on a letting of that property as a whole, that on the termination of the current tenancy you require possession of the holding for the purpose of letting or otherwise disposing of the said property as a whole, and that in view thereof the tenant ought not to be granted a new tenancy;

(f) that on the termination of the current tenancy you intend to demolish or reconstruct the premises comprised in the holding or a substantial part of those premises or to carry out substantial work of construction on the holding or part thereof and that you could not reasonably do so without obtaining possession of the holding;

(If you use this ground, the court can sometimes still grant a new tenancy if certain conditions set out in s 31A of the Act can be met.)

(g) that on the termination of the current tenancy you intend to occupy the holding for the purposes, or partly for the purposes, of a business to be carried on by him therein, or as your residence.

(You must normally have been the landlord for at least five years to use this ground.)

You can only use one or more of the above grounds if you have stated them in the notice referred to in note 2 above.

Compensation

• If your tenant cannot get a new tenancy solely because grounds (e), (f), or (g), apply, he is entitled to compensation from you under the 1954 Act. If you have opposed his application on any of the other grounds as well as (e), (f) or (g), he can only get compensation if the court's refusal to grant a new tenancy is based solely on grounds (e), (f) or (g). In other words, he cannot get compensation under the 1954 Act if the court has refused his tenancy on other grounds even if (e), (f) or (g) also apply.

• If you are an authority possessing compulsory purchase power (such as a local authority) you will be aware that your tenant may be entitled to a disturbance payment under Part III of the Land Compensation Act 1973.

Negotiating a new tenancy

• Most leases are renewed by negotiation. If you do try to agree a new tenancy with your tenant:

  (1) YOU should remember that you will not be able to oppose an application to the court for a new tenancy unless you give the notice mentioned in note 2 above within the time limit in that note;

  (2) YOUR TENANT should remember that he will lose his right to apply to the court for a new tenancy unless he makes the application not less than two nor more than four months after the making of this request.

Validity of this notice

• The landlord to whom this request is made may not be the landlord to whom the tenant pays the rent. 'Business' is given a wide meaning in the 1954 Act and is used in the same sense in this request. The 1954 Act also has rules about the date which the tenant can put in para 3. This depends on the terms of the tenancy. If you have any doubts about whether this request is valid, get immediate advice.

Explanatory booklet

The Department of the Environment and Welsh Office booklet *Business Leases and Security of Tenure* explains the main provisions of Part II of the 1954 Act. It is available from the Department of the Environment Publications Store, Building No 3, Victoria Road, South Ruislip, Middlesex.

9.3.6 Landlord's counter-notice

LANDLORD AND TENANT ACT 1954
SECTION 26(6)

Landlord's Notice Opposing Grant of New
Tenancy of Business Premises

To	*O Limited*
Of	*22 High Row, Marton on Tyne, Northumberland*
I/we received on a new tenancy	*2 January 2001* your request for
of	*22 High Row, Marton on Tyne, Northumberland*

TAKE NOTICE that I/we shall oppose an application to the court for the grant of a new tenancy on the grounds mentioned in paragraph~~(s)~~ *(5)(f)* of s 30(1) of the Landlord and Tenant Act 1954, as set out overleaf in Note 3 to this notice.

DATED	*16 January 2001*
Signed:	*A Solicitor and Co*

[As solicitor/agent for] Landlord

Name of Landlord:	*A Limited*
Address of Landlord:	*1 High Street Worktown*

[Name and address of solicitor/agent:]

A Solicitor and Co
23 High Street
Worktown

NOTES

1   A landlord who wishes to oppose an application to the court by the tenant for a new tenancy must serve this notice within two months of the tenant making his request.

2   The grounds upon which the landlord may oppose an application to the court are limited to those set out in note 3. The landlord can only rely on grounds specified in this notice, by the insertion of the appropriate paragraph letter(s). References to more than one ground may be inserted.

3   The grounds on which the landlord may oppose the tenant's application, as specified in the Landlord and Tenant Act 1954, s 30(1), are:

Grounds

(a) where under the current tenancy the tenant has any obligations as respects the repair and maintenance of the holding, that the tenant ought not to be granted a new tenancy in view of the state of repair of the holding, being a state resulting from the tenant's failure to comply with the said obligations;

(b) that the tenant ought not to be granted a new tenancy in view of his persistent delay in paying rent which has become due;

(c) that the tenant ought not to be granted a new tenancy in view of other substantial breaches by him of his obligations under the current tenancy, or for any other reason connected with the tenant's use or management of the holding;

(d) that the landlord has offered and is willing to provide or secure the provision of alternative accommodation for the tenant, that the terms on which the alternative accommodation is available are reasonable having regard to the terms of the current tenancy and to all other relevant circumstances, and that the accommodation and the time at which it will be available are suitable for the tenant's requirements (including the requirement to preserve goodwill) having regard to the nature and class of his business and to the situation and extent of, and facilities afforded by, the holding;

(e) where the current tenancy was created by the sub-letting of part only of the property comprised in a superior tenancy and the landlord is the owner of an interest in reversion expectant on the termination of that superior tenancy, that the aggregate of the rents reasonably obtainable on separate lettings of the holding and the remainder of that property would be substantially less than the rent reasonably obtainable on a letting of that property as a whole, that on the termination of the current tenancy the landlord requires possession of the holding for the purposes of letting or otherwise disposing of the said property as a whole, and that in view thereof the tenant ought not to be granted a new tenancy;

(f) that on the termination of the current tenancy the landlord intends to demolish or reconstruct the premises comprised in the holding or a substantial part of those premises or to carry out substantial work of construction on the holding or part thereof and that he could not reasonably do so without obtaining possession of the holding;

(g) that on the termination of the current tenancy the landlord intends to occupy the holding for the purposes, or partly for the purposes, of a business to be carried on by him therein, or as his residence.

4   In s 30(1), quoted in note 3, 'the holding' means the property comprised in the tenancy, other than any which is occupied neither by the tenant nor by someone whom he employs for the purposes of a business which brings the tenancy within the scope of the Landlord and Tenant Act 1954, s 23(3).

9.3.7 Form N397 – Application for new tenancy under Pt II of the Landlord and Tenant Act 1954

IN THE *Marton on Tyne* COUNTY COURT

No of MATTER XY 12345

In the matter of the Landlord and Tenant Act 1954 and

In the matter of *the lease of the premises known as 22 High Row, Marton upon Tyne, Northumberland*

Between

<table>
<tr><td></td><td>O Limited</td><td>Applicant</td></tr>
<tr><td></td><td>– and –</td><td></td></tr>
<tr><td></td><td>A Limited</td><td>Respondent</td></tr>
</table>

1   [I] [We]   *O Limited*
    of   *22 High Row, Marton on Tyne, Northumberland*
    apply to the court for the grant of a new tenancy pursuant to Part II of the Landlord and Tenant Act 1954.

2   The premises to which this application relates are [is]:–
    22 High Row, Marton on Tyne, Northumberland

3   The nature of the business carried on at the premises:–
    a newsagents and confectioner's shop

4   The following are the particulars of our current tenancy of the premises:–

(a) (Date of lease or agreement for a lease or tenancy agreement)
    1 April 1995

(b) (Names of parties to lease or agreement)
    A Limited (1) and O Limited (2)

(c) (Term granted by lease or agreement)
    five years from and including 1 July 1996

(d) (Rent reserved by lease or agreement)
    £8,000 per annum

(e) (Terms as to date and mode of termination of tenancy)
    Break clause exercisable by landlord serving not less than three months' notice expiring on 31 October 1998 and usual rights of re-entry upon tenant's breach of covenant.

(f) (Whether any and, if so, what part of the property comprised in the tenancy is occupied neither by the tenant, nor by a person employed by the tenant for the purposes of the business carried on by the tenant in the premises)

None

(ALTERNATIVE WHERE LANDLORD SERVED A s 25 NOTICE (9.3.3))

5   On *2 January 2001* the Respondent served on us a notice to terminate dated *1 January 2001* in accordance with the provisions of s 25 of the 1954 Act specifying *5 July 2001* as the date for termination and stating that the Respondent would [not] oppose an application to this court for a new tenancy.

On *17 January 2001* We served on the Respondent:

a counter-notice dated *16 January 2001* stating that We would not be willing to give up possession of the premises on the date of termination.]

(ALTERNATIVE WHERE TENANT SERVED A s 26 REQUEST (9.3.5))

5.   On *2 January 2001* We served on the Respondent a request dated *1 January 2001* for a new tenancy in accordance with the provisions of s 26 of the Act specifying 30 December 2001 as the date for the commencement of the new tenancy. (3) [The Respondent has not served on us any counter-notice. [On *17 January 2001* the Respondent served on us a counter-notice dated *16 January 2001* stating that it would oppose an application to the court for the grant of a new tenancy.]]

6   The following are our proposals as to the period, rent and other terms of the new tenancy for which we are applying:

> *A term of five years at a rent of £10,000 per annum with a break clause exercisable by either party serving not less than three months' notice on the other expiring at the end of the third year of the term but otherwise on the same terms as the current tenancy.*

7   The following persons are to our knowledge interested in reversion in the premises on the termination of our current tenancy:

None

8   The following other persons have to [my][our] knowledge an interest in the premises other than a freehold interest and are likely to be affected by the grant of a new tenancy:

9 The name and address of the Defendant on whom this application is intended to be served are:

10 Our address for service is:

11 Statement of Truth

[(6) (I believe)(The Applicant believes) that the facts stated in the originating application are true].

[(6) I am duly authorised by the Applicant to sign this statement].

Full name.....................................

Name of Applicant's Solicitor's firm

Signed   position or office held

(Applicant) (Applicant's solicitor)   (if signing on behalf of firm or company)

Dated this   *8th*   day of   *April 2001*

Commentary

It should be noted that the recent Consultation Paper (see above, 4.1) proposes that, in future, all claims made under the 1954 Act will begin in the county court and that the appropriate claim form will be part 7 unless the claim is:

• for interim rent under s 24A of the 1954 Act made by the landlord before the tenant has begun a claim for a new tenancy – in which case Part 8 will apply;

• to authorise an agreement made under s 38(4) of the 1954 Act to exclude the operation of the renewal provisions in the 1954 Act – in which case Part 8 will be used.

In the meantime, the procedure in the county court is principally governed by:

• section B of the second practice direction to Part 8 (PD 8B);

• CCR Ord 43, rr 6–15.

It should be noted that, although the primary source of the procedure is PD 8B, the claim is not, in fact, a Part 8 claim. CCR Ord 43 still uses the terms applicant and respondent, although PD 8B refers to the parties as claimant and defendant. The proceedings are commenced by claim form (CCR Ord 43, r 2(1)). The correct form is N397, the old form which was used before the CPR came into force.

The CPR state that the claim may only be started in the county court for the district in which:

- the defendant (that is, the landlord) or one of the defendants lives or carries on business, or
- the subject matter of the claim is situated (PD 8B, B.6 (1)).

If proceedings have been started in the wrong court, a judge may order that they:

- be transferred to the county court in which they ought to have been started;
- continue in the county court in which they have been started; or
- be struck out (CPR 30.2(2)).

An application for such an order must be made in the county court where the claim is proceeding (CPR 30.2(3)).

In making the application, the applicant files in the appropriate court:

- a self-addressed envelope where issuing through the post;
- a request;
- Form N397 and copy for each other party;
- a cheque for £120;
- a request for service to be made by the claimant (if required).

If the claimant does not request service, the court will automatically serve a notice and copy of the application upon the defendant by first class post (CCR Ord 7, r 10(1) and Ord 3, r 4(6)). Where the papers are served by the court, the date of service shall, unless the contrary is shown, be deemed to be the seventh day after the date on which the application was sent to the respondent (CCR Ord 7, r 10(3)). The application must be served within two months of its issue or within such further period as the court may allow (CCR Ord 7, r 20(1) and (2) and Ord 43, r 6(3)). The claim must be served in time. If, following judgment or the making of an order, it appears to the court that the process did not come to the notice of the respondent in time, the judgment or order can be set aside (CCR Ord 37, r 3). Personal service may therefore be preferred rather than relying on postal service by an officer of the court.

When the court issues the claim, it should also fix a hearing date. The first hearing will be a case management conference.

9.3.8 Landlord's answer

IN THE *Marton on Tyne* COUNTY COURT

No of MATTER XY 12345

In the matter of the Landlord and Tenant Act 1954 and

In the matter of *the lease of the premises known as 22 High Row Marton on Tyne Northumberland*

Between

O Limited	Applicant
– and –	
A Limited	Respondent

WE,   *A Limited*

of   *1 High Street Worktown Northumberland*

the respondent in this matter, in answer to the application of *O Limited* for a new tenancy of the premises known as *22 High Row Marton on Tyne Northumberland* say that:–

1   We do not oppose the grant of a new tenancy

We oppose the grant of a new tenancy on the following grounds stated in our notice under section [25] [26(6)] of the Act, namely:

> *The ground mentioned in paragraph (f) of s 30(1) of the Act.*

2   If a new tenancy is granted we do not object to its being granted on the terms proposed by the Applicant.

If a new tenancy is granted, we object to its being granted on the following terms proposed by the Applicant, namely:–

> *A rent of £10,000 per annum and a break clause exercisable by either party serving not less than three months' notice on the other expiring at the end of the third year of the term*

and the following are our counter-proposals as to the period, rent and other terms of such a tenancy:

> *A rent of £15,000 per annum and a break clause exercisable only by the landlord serving not less than three months' notice expiring at the end of the third year of the term but otherwise on the same terms as the current tenancy.*

3   We are not a tenant under a lease having less than 14 years unexpired at the date of termination of the Applicant's current tenancy.

[We are a tenant under a lease having less than 14 years unexpired at the date of termination of the Applicant's current tenancy, and the name and address of the person(s) having an interest in the reversion expectant on the termination of the Respondent's tenancy immediately or within not more than 14 years of the date of such termination [is] [are]:]

4   The following persons are to our knowledge likely to be affected by the grant of a new tenancy:

None

[5   We require that any new tenancy ordered to be granted shall be a tenancy of the whole of the property comprised in the Applicant's current tenancy.]

6   We hereby apply to the court under s 24A of the Act to determine a rent which would be reasonable for the Applicant to pay while the tenancy continues by virtue of s 24 of the Act.

Dated this   *30*   day of   *April 2001*

A Solicitor and Co

Solicitor for the Respondent

Commentary

By virtue of PD 8B, para B12, the landlord is not required to serve an acknowledgment of service, but must file an answer (CCR Ord 43, r 2(1)). The date upon which this must be done is not stated, but given that the first hearing will be a case management conference, the answer should be filed well in advance so that appropriate directions can be given and the case advanced. The contents of the answer are prescribed by CCR Ord 43, r 7.

The answer should be accompanied by as many copies as there are other parties to the proceedings (CCR Ord 9, r 18(3)). The court will send a copy to the applicant and to every other party (CCR Ord 9, r 18(4)).

9.3.9 Form N279 – Notice of discontinuance

Note: Where another party must consent to the proceedings being discontinued, a copy of their consent must be attached to, and served with, this form	In the *Marton on Tyne County Court*	
	Claim No	*XY 12345*
	Claimant (including ref)	*O Limited*
	Defendant (including ref)	*A Limited*

To the court

The claimant (defendant)   *O Limited*

(tick only one box)

✓	discontinues all of this (claim) (counterclaim)
☐	discontinues that part of this claim (counterclaim) relating to: *(specify which part)*

against the (defendant) (following defendants) (claimants) (following claimants)

(........................ *(enter name of Judge)* granted permission for the claimant to discontinue (all) (part) of this (claim) (counterclaim) by order dated ....)

I certify that I have served a copy of this notice on every other party to the proceedings

Signed _____   (Claimant)
(Defendant)('s solicitor)
(Litigation friend)

Position or office held _____   (if signing on behalf of firm or company)

Date _____

Commentary

A tenant who has decided not to pursue its application for a new lease may discontinue proceedings under CPR Pt 38. The discontinuance 'takes effect on the date when notice of discontinuance is served' on the defendant under CPR, r 38.3 (see CPR, r 38.5). The defendant may apply to have the notice of discontinuance set aside (CPR, r 38.4), but subject to that right 'the proceedings are brought to an end as against him on that date'. In a lease renewal claim, this means that the tenancy will come to an end three months after service of the notice (see s 64 of the 1954 Act), so that the tenant will remain liable to pay rent (including interim rent, if applied for by the landlord) until then. There are certain cases where permission to discontinue is required, for example, where the court has granted an interim injunction, but they are unlikely to apply in lease renewal claims (CPR, r 38.2).

Unless the court otherwise orders, the landlord is entitled to his costs incurred on or before the date the notice is served (CPR, r 38.6). If the tenant wishes to discontinue because a new tenancy has been granted by agreement, Precedent 9.3.10 is preferable, as it deals expressly both with costs and the landlord's application for interim rent.

9.3.10 Consent Order dismissing tenant's application for a new lease

IN THE *Marton on Tyne* COUNTY COURT

No of MATTER XY 12345

In the matter of the Landlord and Tenant Act 1954 and

In the matter of the lease of the premises known as *22 High Row*
Marton on Tyne
Northumberland

Between

O Limited   Applicant

– and –

A Limited   Respondent

CONSENT ORDER

BY CONSENT IT IS ORDERED THAT:

1 The Claim herein be dismissed with no Order as to costs.

2 The Defendant's Application under *s 24A* Landlord and Tenant Act 1954 for the determination of an interim rent be dismissed with no Order as to costs.

....

Hopitees   *Messrs A Solicitor and Co*
The Towers   *23 High Street*
Worktown   *Worktown*
Northumberland   *Northumberland*

Solicitors for the Applicant   Solicitors for the Respondent

Notes

It would be appropriate to use this form of consent order to dismiss the outstanding court proceedings once a new tenancy has been granted by agreement. An agreement on interim rent also needs to have been reached, otherwise para 2 is inappropriate.

The order provides expressly that there will be no costs order (that is, each party will bear its own costs). This is usual where a negotiated settlement has been reached.

9.4   Licence permitting assignment

THIS LICENCE is made the   *First day of January 2001*

BETWEEN the party whose name and address is set out in Part I of the FIRST SCHEDULE hereto ('the Landlord') of the first part the party whose name and address is set out in Part II of that Schedule ('the Tenant') of the second part and the party whose name and address is set out in Part III of that Schedule ('the Assignee') of the third part and is SUPPLEMENTAL to the Lease ('the Lease') referred to in the SECOND SCHEDULE hereto whereby the premises ('the Premises') briefly described in that Schedule were demised for the term of years ('the Term') referred to in that Schedule subject to the payment of the rents reserved by and the performance and observance of the covenants on the lessee's part and the conditions contained in the Lease.

Now this Deed witnesseth as follows:

1   The Landlord grants to the Tenant licence to assign all the estate and interest of the Tenant in the Premises to the Assignee.

[2   The Assignee covenants with the Landlord that as from the date of the assignment and throughout the residue of the Term the Assignee will pay the rents and other sums of money reserved and made payable by the Lease including increased rent arising on review pursuant to the provisions in that behalf contained in the Lease and observe and perform the covenants on the part of the lessee and the conditions therein contained and will indemnify the Landlord against all actions costs losses claims demands and liabilities arising from any non-payment of the rents or any non-observance or non-performance of the covenants and conditions.]

3   The Tenant covenants with the Landlord that the Tenant will pay the Landlord's reasonable and proper costs of and in connection with this Deed including those arising from the consideration of the application for and preparation and completion of this Deed.

4   If the assignment hereby authorised shall not have been implemented and the Deed of Assignment or a certified copy thereof produced to the Landlord's Solicitors within two months from the date hereof then the Landlord is entitled by giving written notice to the Tenant and the Assignee to terminate this Licence at any time thereafter but termination does not oblige the Landlord to refund any payments made under Clause 3 nor prejudice any accrued right of action vested in the Landlord or arising from any earlier breach by the Tenant of its obligations under this Licence.

5   The proviso for re-entry contained in the Lease shall be exercisable by the Landlord as well on breach by the Assignee of any of the provisions herein contained as on the happening of any of the events mentioned in such proviso.

6   In this Licence where the context admits the expression 'the Landlord' shall include the persons from time to time entitled in reversion immediately expectant on the Term and the expression 'the Assignee' shall include the persons deriving title under the Assignee and where the expressions 'the Tenant' and 'the Assignee' comprise two or more persons the obligations of the Tenant and the Assigned respectively shall be construed as joint and several.

THIS LICENCE is executed as a Deed and is delivered on the date stated at the beginning of this Deed

THE FIRST SCHEDULE

Part I (the Landlord)

HORACE SCOTT of Viewforth Ashtown North Yorkshire

Part II (the Tenant)

ALICE WHITE of 4 Town View Ashtown North Yorkshire

Part III (the Assignee)

JENNIFER FROCK of 36 Milburn Street Ashtown North Yorkshire

THE SECOND SCHEDULE

Particulars of the Lease

Date:	*29 September 1973*
The parties:	*Horace Scott (1) and Neville Shepherd (2)*
The premises:	*113 High Row Ashtown North Yorkshire*
The term:	*25 years*

SIGNED AS A DEED

by the said   *HORACE SCOTT*

in the presence of:

SIGNED AS A DEED

by the said   *ALICE WHITE*

in the presence of:

SIGNED AS A DEED

by the said   *JENNIFER FROCK*

in the presence of:

Commentary

If the lease being assigned is a new tenancy as defined by the 1995 Act (see 3.1), clause 2 is unnecessary (see 3.1.8) and almost certainly void by virtue of the anti-avoidance provisions of the 1995 Act (see 3.1.9). It should therefore be omitted.

If the lease being assigned is an old tenancy, clause 2 is necessary since, without it, the Assignee would only be liable for breaches of the covenants in the lease (touching and concerning the premises) occurring during her period of ownership.

9.5 Notice of arrears under the 1995 Act

NOTICE TO FORMER TENANT OR GUARANTOR
OF INTENTION TO RECOVER FIXED CHARGE (1)

(Landlord and Tenant (Covenants) Act 1995, s 17)

To [name and address]: **Alice White**

of   **4 Town View, Ashtown, North Yorkshire**

Important – The person giving this notice is protecting the right
to recover the amount(s) specified from you now or at some time
in the future. There may be action which you can take to protect
your position. read the notice and all the notes overleaf carefully.
If you are in any doubt about the action you should take, seek
advice immediately eg from a solicitor or citizens advice bureau.

---

1   This notice is given under s 17 of the Landlord and Tenant (Covenants)
Act 1995 (see note 1 below).

2   It relates to (address and description of property) **113 High Row,
Ashtown, North Yorkshire**

let under a lease dated **29 September 1973** and made between
Horace Scott (1) and **Neville Shepherd (2)**

[of which you were formerly tenant] [in relation to which you are
liable as guarantor of a person who was formerly tenant]. (2)

3   I/we as landlord (3) hereby give you notice that the fixed charge(s)
of which details are set out in the attached Schedule (4) is/are now
due and unpaid, and that I/we intend to recover from you the amount(s)
specified in the Schedule [and interest from the date and calculated
on the basis specified in the Schedule] (5) (see notes 2 and 3 below).

4   (6) There is a possibility that your liability in respect of the fixed
charge(s) detailed in the Schedule will subsequently be determined
to be for a greater amount (see note 4 below).

5   All correspondence about this notice should be sent to the
landlord/landlord's agent at the address given below.

Date **1 January 2001**

Signature of landlord/landlord's agent

Name and address of landlord **Horace Scott of Viewforth, Ashtown,
North Yorkshire**

[Name and address of agent *Z Solicitor and Co, High Street, Ashtown, North Yorkshire*]

SCHEDULE

Date due	Amount	Type of payment
25 March 2000	*£5,000.00*	*Rent*

together with interest payable at the rate of 10% per annum on and from *25 March 2000* until the date of payment in accordance with clause 3(2) of the lease.

NOTES

1   The person giving you this notice alleges that you are still liable for the performance of the tenant's obligations under the tenancy to which this notice relates, either as a previous tenant bound by privity of contract or an authorised guarantee agreement, or because you are the guarantor of a previous tenant. By giving you this notice, the landlord (or other person entitled to enforce payment, such as a management company) is protecting his right to require you to pay the amount specified in the notice. There may be other sums not covered by the notice which the landlord can also recover because they are not fixed charges (for example, in respect of repairs or costs if legal proceedings have to be brought). If you pay the amount specified in this notice in full, you will have the right to call on the landlord to grant you an 'overriding lease', which puts you in the position of landlord to the present tenant. There are both advantages and drawbacks to doing this, and you should take advice before coming to a decision.

Validity of notice

2   The landlord is required to give this notice within six months of the date on which the charge or charges in question became due (or, if it became due before 1 January 1996, within six months of that date). If the notice has been given late, it is not valid, and the amount in the notice cannot be recovered from you. The date of the giving of the notice may not be the date written on the notice or the date on which you actually saw it. It may, for instance, be the date on which the notice was delivered through the post to your last address known to the landlord. If you are in any doubt, you should seek advice immediately.

Interest

3   If interest is payable on the amount due, the landlord does not have to state the precise amount of interest, but he must state the basis on which the interest is calculated to enable you to work out the likely amount, or he will not be able to claim interest at all. This does not include interest which may be payable under rules of court if legal proceedings are brought.

Change in amount due

4   Apart from interest, the landlord is not entitled to recover an amount which is more than he has specified in the notice, with one exception. This is where the amount cannot be finally determined within six months after it is due (for example, if there is dispute concerning an outstanding rent review or if the charge is a service charge collected on account and adjusted following final determination). In such a case, if the amount due is eventually determined to be more than originally notified, the landlord may claim the larger amount if, and only if, he completes the paragraph giving notice of the possibility that the amount may change, and gives a further notice specifying the larger amount within three months of the final determination.

Footnotes:

1   The Act defines a fixed charge as (a) rent, (b) any service charge (as defined by s 18 of the Landlord and Tenant Act 1985, disregarding the words 'of a dwelling') and (c) any amount payable under a tenant covenant of the tenancy providing for payment of a liquidated sum in the event of failure to comply with the covenant.

2   Delete alternative as appropriate.

3   'Landlord' for these purposes includes any person who has the right to enforce the charge.

4   The Schedule must be in writing, and must indicate in relation to each item the date on which it became payable, the amount payable and whether it is rent, service charge or a fixed charge of some other kind (in which case, particulars of the nature of the charge should be given). Charges due before 1 January 1996 are deemed to have become due on that date, but the actual date on which they became due should also be stated.

5   Delete words in brackets if not applicable. If applicable, the Schedule must state the basis on which interest is calculated (for example, rate of interest, date from which it is payable and provision of Lease or other document under which it is payable).

6 Delete this paragraph if not applicable. If applicable (for example, where there is an outstanding rent review or service charge collected on account), a further notice must be served on the former tenant or guarantor within three (3) months beginning with the date on which the greater amount is determined. If only applicable to one or more charge of several, the Schedule should specify which.

Commentary

This form is based on a claim for arrears under the lease assigned under the precedent licence set out in 9.4, which is an old tenancy (see 3.1.2). The notice assumes that the assignee has not paid the rent due on 25 March 1999.

The form of the Schedule attached to the notice is not prescribed: footnote 4 sets out the requirements for the Schedule.

See 3.1.5 for details of the provisions of s 17 of the 1995 Act, under which this notice is required.

10 Further Reading

10.1 Looseleaf works

Such works have become popular in recent years and are regularly updated. They now include:

Adams, JE, *Precedents for the Conveyancer*, London: Sweet & Maxwell

Aldridge, T, *Leasehold Law*, London: Sweet & Maxwell

Aldridge, T, *Practical Conveyancing Precedents*, London: Sweet & Maxwell★

Aldridge, T, *Practical Lease Precedents*, London: Sweet & Maxwell★

Farrand, JT and Clarke, A, *Emmet on Title*, London: Sweet & Maxwell★

Furber, J (Gen ed), Hill and Redman, *Law of Landlord and Tenant*, London: Butterworths★

Kenny, P, Kenny, A and Alexander, J, *Sweet & Maxwell's Conveyancing Practice*, London: Sweet & Maxwell

Reynolds, K, Featherstonhaugh, G and Bernstein, R, *Handbook of Rent Review*, London: Sweet & Maxwell

Ross, MJ, *Commercial Leases*, 5th edn, 1998, London: Butterworths

Williams, D, Brand, C and Hubbard, C, *Handbook of Business Tenancies*, London: Sweet & Maxwell

Woodfall, *Landlord and Tenant*, London: Sweet & Maxwell ★

All of the above works are excellent and a selection, taking into account the fact that some cover similar ground, should be on all practitioners' shelves. Those marked with an asterisk are also available on CD-ROM.

10.2 Books

The following books may prove useful, especially those marked with an asterisk:

*Aldridge, T, *Letting Business Premises*, 7th edn, 1996, London: Sweet & Maxwell

Bamford, K, *Commercial Property: Amending a Commercial Lease*, 1998, London: Butterworths

Bernstein, R and Reynolds, K, *Essentials of Rent Review*, 1995, London: Sweet & Maxwell

Brand, C, *Planning Law*, 4th edn, 2001, London: Cavendish Publishing

*Butterworths, *Business Landlord and Tenant Handbook*, 2nd edn, 1998, London: Butterworths

*Coates, R, *Conveyancing*, 4th edn, 2001, London: Cavendish Publishing

Encyclopaedia of Forms and Precedents, Vol 22, 5th edn, 1999 re-issue, London: Butterworths

Fancourt, T, *Enforceability of Landlord and Tenant Covenants*, 1997, London: Sweet & Maxwell

Freedman, P, *Interpreting and Enforcing Commercial Leases*, 1998, Bristol: Jordans

Hilditch, B and Fife, G *Renewing Business Tenancies*, 1998, Bristol: Jordans

Furber, J (Gen ed), *Hill and Redman's Guide to Landlord and Tenant Law*, 1999, London: Butterworths

Kemp, M, *Drafting and Negotiating Rent Review Clauses*, London: Sweet & Maxwell

Lewison, K, *Drafting Business Leases*, 5th edn, 1996, London: Sweet & Maxwell

*Sweet & Maxwell's Directory of Local Authorities, 2000

Reynolds, K and Bernstein, R, *Renewal of Business Tenancies*, 2nd edn, 2001, London: Sweet & Maxwell

Silverman, F, *Standard Conditions of Sale: A Conveyancer's Guide*, 6th edn, 1999, London: Butterworths Tolley

Sweet, R, *Commercial Leases: Tenants' Amendments*, 3rd edn, 1998, London: Sweet & Maxwell

10.2 Journals

The *Estates Gazette* is essential reading for anyone specialising in this area of law, as it is a specialist landlord and tenant journal. The *Law Society's Gazette* and *Solicitors' Journal* are also useful, as is *Rent Review and Lease Renewal*.

10.4 Websites

The Civil Procedure Rules and the associated Practice Directions and other material are made available by the Lord Chancellor's Department and Court Service, usually in an HTML version, but sometimes in PDF or a word processing format. The forms are interactive, in that they may be completed on screen, printed off and sent to the court.

The Court Service is at http://www.courtservice.gov.uk/ and the Lord Chancellor's Department is at www.open.gov.uk/lcd.

The RICS website at www.RICS.org.uk contains information on rent reviews and PACT. A very helpful and accessible site which includes updated information about the lease renewal procedure is www.garywebber.co.uk.

Archived copies of the Law Society's Gazette at located at www.lawgazette.co.uk.